The Hogmanay Companion

Hugh Douglas

The Hogmanay Companion

Hugh Douglas
Illustrations by Keith Horrox

Neil Wilson Publishing • Glasgow

© Hugh Douglas, 1993

Published by Neil Wilson Publishing Ltd
309 The Pentagon Centre
36 Washington Street
GLASGOW G3 8AZ
Tel: 041-221-1117
Fax: 041-221-5363

A catalogue record for this book is available from The British Library
ISBN 1-897784-12-0

Typeset in 12/13pt Times New Roman
by Face to Face Design Services, Glasgow

Printed in Musselburgh by Scotprint Ltd

To all my family and
the many, many friends
who have shared Hogmanays
in Scotland and in England
over the years.

To Ane and A'
A Guid New Year and mony o' them!

Other books written by the author:

Robert Burns — A Life
The Burns Supper Companion
Flora Macdonald — The Most Loyal Rebel
The Underground Story
Crossing the Forth
Portrait of the Burns Country
Edinburgh, A Children's Story
Burke and Hare, The True Story
Charles Edward Stuart — The Man, The King, The Legend
Minishant is a Bonnie Wee Place
(with Henrietta Douglas)

Contents

Acknowledgements

Many people have shared their Hogmanay memories to help compile this book. Friends and people I have met only on paper have generously told me about New Year as it was and is celebrated in their families and in their areas. They have given me rhymes, rites and recipes galore. My grateful thanks to all of them, but especially Sheena Ambrose, the late John MacInnes, Dan Murray and John Douglas.

Libraries and newspapers from Lerwick to Guernsey have helped to discover sources which I could never have located wthout them. As a single example, a letter to *The Oban Times* brought a reply from Mrs M Powell, a Gaelic speaker who lives no more than a mile from my own home in Peterborough! She has given great assistance with translation.

I am grateful to Jenny Moser, Isabelle Shaw, Mary Campbell, my sisters Amelia Gregor and Margaret Skilling, and other members of my family who have delved into their recipes to provide the substance for much of appendix 1.

My thanks also to Keith Horrox who provided the illustrations which enliven the text and to Sue Sharpe and Margaret McEwen who typed it.

Although the Scottish Hogmanay is well documented through Mrs M MacLeod's *British Calendar Customs* and F Marian McNeill's *The Silver Bough* and other books, the festival has altered in character and is still undergoing change. I am pleased to say that although many correspondents have expressed fears that Hogmanay is dying, I can reassure them that it is alive and well and living, not just in Scotland, but wherever Scots are to be found around the world.

Hugh Douglas, August 1993

Part One

Why Hogmanay?

*'But surely you haven't had a good
New Year if you can remember it.'*

*Response of a correspondent on
being asked for Hogmanay memories*

In Scotland we call it Hogmanay; to the English and the rest of the world it's New Year's Eve, except in America where they don't take time to say even that. They abbreviate the name of the last day of the year to New Year's, or is it New Years? New Year's or New Years indeed! Do they mean New Year's *something*, or several new years rolled into one glorious binge?

In Scotland there is no such confusion — you know where you are on Hogmanay, which is usually with friends, glass in hand, toasting the year departing and the year beginning, which you always feel sure will be better than the one being left behind.

Only one person matters in Scotland at New Year — the first to cross the threshold after midnight, the 'first-foot'. Not just anybody will do to fill this important role because this first visitor of the year brings all the luck, good or bad, which the household will encounter during the twelve months ahead.

The first-footer should be a tall dark man without a limp, stammer, or other physical handicap and he must carry a lump of coal to signify warmth and comfort, cake to denote plenty and a bottle, preferably of whisky, from which to pour a dram to toast the health of all who live in the house. A silver coin would not go amiss to ensure prosperity as well.

People in other countries may laugh this custom off as silly super-

stition, but Scots, even those who would ridicule such beliefs at other times, are careful to observe it to the letter. Celebrating Hogmanay is a serious business.

The last stroke of midnight on the last day of the year is a very special point in any Scot's life, a watershed, a turning of the tide, the opening of a dam to release all the tainted waters of the past twelve months and allow a pure new stream of life to flow in. It is the start of a journey into a pristine, unsullied year.

Hogmanay is known by several different names. Because people once went round the doors on New Year's Eve guising for food, it was known as Cake Day, a name still alive in parts of Scotland and in the north of England. In the east it used to be called Singing E'en because of the custom of singing Yule carols, but this name has died out, and no one to whom I have spoken in either Fife or Angus (the counties where it was once used) can remember it. Older folk sometimes call the last night of the year Old Year's Night.

In pre-Reformation Gaelic-speaking Scotland Christmas Eve was *Oidhche Choinnle*, 'the Night of the Candles', and to this day on the Catholic islands of the Hebrides they put candles in their windows on that night. Protestant islands appropriated the name for Hogmanay. They also call New Year's Eve *Oidhche na Challuinne*, 'the Night of the New Year'. New Year's Day is *Oidhche nam Bannag*, 'the Night of the Bannocks'.

In the Shetland Islands New Year is called Yules, demonstrating the enduring Viking influence in those northern isles, which lie nearer to Norway than to Edinburgh.

Hogmanay means more than the eve of the New Year: the word is used for the presents given and received at that time, and in some places it is a general name for the whole New Year festival.

But what does the word *Hogmanay* really mean, and where did it originate?

Dr John Jamieson in his *Etymological Dictionary of the Scottish Language* published in 1808-9 wrote that Hogmanay was "the name appropriated by the vulgar to the last day of the year". This is of little help: we all know it is a word adopted by the commonman for the last day of the year, but Jamieson and others have little to say on the derivation. 'Origin obscure' is the most they will tell you.

Although Hogmanay is the accepted spelling today, it varied enormously in the old days; from *hag-me-nay* in Galloway to *huggeranohni* in Shetland. The *English Dialect Dictionary* gives no fewer than seventeen spelling variations, to which the *Scottish National Dictionary* adds a further fourteen. However, spelling is no help since the word was handed down by word of mouth through countless generations.

The *Scottish National Dictionary* traces the word back to 1696 and a reference to poor women singing 'a hog ma nae song'. Joseph Wright's *English Dialect Dictionary* cites another reference from the same year, telling us, 'It is ordinary among some plebeians to go about from door to door upon New Year's eve, crying Hagmana, a corrupted word from the Greek *Hagia-mana*, which signifies the *holy month*.' The *Oxford English Dictionary* takes the word back a little further, to 1680, when it was listed among the various festivals, 'Pasch-Sunday, Hallow-even, Hogmynae-night and Valentines-even'.

All this is very interesting and sheds a little light on how Hogmanay was celebrated, but, Greek apart, it does not bring us nearer to a derivation. Ancient Greece's claim with *Hagia-mana* is disputed by several other languages. Without leaving Scotland, one can cite a Gaelic Hogmanay song which opens with the words, *oge maidne*, meaning *new morning*. Head across the Border and the Venerable Bede wrote of a *Haleg monath* or holy month; alas, his holy month was September, not December.

Scandinavians, who exercised great influence in the Hebrides and other parts of Scotland for centuries, stake their claim with *Hoggo-nott*, *Hogenat* or *Hogg-night*, the ancient Scandinavian name for the night preceding the feast of Yule. The word *hagg* means *to kill* or *to cut* and is said to derive from the custom of slaughtering animals for the Yule feast. An Englishman, Christopher Clarkson, in his history of the town of Richmond in Yorkshire, also links it to Scandinavia through a North Country word related to the Scandinavian verb *hagg*. *Hagman Heigh*, he said, had some connection with a woodcutter or hagman who brought in the Yule logs.

An old German claim is similar, using the word to *hogg* or *to kill*, and *minne* which is *remembrance*. Squeezing both words into a linguistic straitjacket this gives Hogmanay the meaning, 'Remember your sacrifices on the feast of Thor'.

Charles Mackay who compiled a *Dictionary of Lowland Scotch*, favours Flemish. 'Nobody has ever thought of looking to the Flemish, which has supplied so many words to the Lowland Scotch, for a solution to the difficulty,' he wrote. 'In that language we find three words: "*hoog*" (*high* or *great*), "*min*" (*love* or *affection*) and "*dag*" (a *day*). "Hoog-min-dag", the high or great day of affection. The transition to hog-man-ay is easily accomplished.'

From Denmark Thorleif Repp, brought a derivation stemming from ancient Norse fairy lore and related to the Hogmanay rhyme:

> *Hogmanay. Trololay.*
> *Gie me some o' your white bread,*
> *An' none o' your grey.*

New Year was the only time in the whole year when the wicked trolls were able to leave the hills in which they lived and come among humans, so Repp believed the words Hogmanay Trololay could be translated from the Norse as, 'Good elves forever and wicked Trolls into the sea,' or in today's parlance — up with the elves; down with the trolls!

The French must have the strongest, almost irresistible claim to both the word and the occasion. There are several possible derivations linked to French, the simplest of which is quoted by Robert Chambers in *The Book of Days*:

> *Homme est né,*
> *Trois rois là.*

That is to say,

> *A man is born,*
> *Three Kings are there.*

This conveniently (or perhaps inconveniently for those who want to keep the two festivals apart), links the Hogmanay festival to Christmas.

Another French theory takes us back to the Middle Ages. In old France there was a custom very similar in name and style to our Hogmanay, and it has been widely accepted that the Scottish Hogmanay was brought over from France with the many other words and observances derived from that Auld Alliance, which linked Scotland and France for hundreds of years.

In France the last day of the old year and the gifts given then were called *aguillaneuf*. On the first day of the year the poor in Brittany went out to collect New Year's gifts with shouts of '*Au gui l'an neuf*'. In Normandy the word was *hoguinelo* and the presents given on that day were *hoguignetes*.

On the Channel Island of Guernsey, they had a word, *oguinani* or *oguinano*, now obsolete. Like children in Scotland and the north of England, young people on the island had a rhyme which they chanted at every door:

> *Oguinani! Oguinano!*
> *Ouvre ta pouque, et pis la recilios.*

This meant 'Oguinani! Oguinano! Open your purse and then shut it,' but before they closed their purses the good Guernsey wives were expected to take out a few coppers to give to the children.

A similar custom common in Spain centuries ago was called *aguinaldo* and the New Year's Day mass there was known as the Aguinaldo Mass.

Au gui l'an neuf is a very tempting derivation since *gui* is the French word for mistletoe and from the dawn of history, mistletoe was considered a sacred plant, with healing properties, which formed part of ancient rituals carried out around the time of the winter solstice in many parts of Europe. Hogmanay may well be a corruption of '*au gui l'an neuf*', meaning 'to the mistletoe of the new year', although the *Oxford English Dictionary* was scornful of this mistletoe derivation. 'These explanations with the reference to the gui or mistletoe are now rejected by French scholars as merely popular etymology.' it stated loftily. 'The alleged French cry, "*au gui menez, tir liri, mainte du blanc et point du bis*" cited secondhand in Jamieson (*Etymological Dictionary of the Scottish Language*) is not to be found in the French author from whom it professes to be quoted and appears to be a figment.'

Perhaps so, but the chant '*Au gui, menez, tir liri, mainte du blanc et point du bis*,' closely resembles 'Hogmanay, trololay, give us your white bread and none of your grey.' *Blanc* could easily refer to white bread which was only eaten on special occasions and *bis* to dark, coarse, every day loaves.

Who is right? Nobody knows the derivation any more than they can identify the true source of Hogmanay itself or the customs and superstitions in which it is enfolded. However, it is difficult to escape from the French Hogmanay connection in one form or another.

The Daft Days

*'The town's bell rang through the dark of
the winter morning with queer little jolts
and pauses...the burgh town turned over on
its pillows...and knew by that bell it was
the daftest of the daft days to come'.*

The Daft Days, Neil Munro

The origins of Scotland's Hogmanay are easier to find than the parentage of the word itself. The sun was the source of power, warmth and even of life itself for early man: he depended on it to provide light, food and fire to sustain life, it enriched his land and it ripened his harvest. The sun therefore was to be feared and worshipped, a god who had to be propitiated.

In autumn man watched the sun moving away and losing its strength to create a time of danger and deprivation; then, just when the days were shortest and darkest and it seemed that this source of life was leaving forever, there came the winter solstice when the sun paused, then slowly started to return, bringing with it the warmth and burgeoning of spring.

This turning point of the year was celebrated with feasting, drinking, sacrifices and special rites to bring good fortune and appease the powerful sun god. Even after the sun ceased to be worshipped, a celebration continued to be held at mid-winter to lighten the darkest days of the year. The Romans called their festival, lasting from the middle of December until the twenty-fourth day of the month, the Saturnalia. Their great day was named *Dies Natalis Solis Invicta*, the 'Birthday of the Unconquered Sun'.

This day continued to be a focal point of the winter celebration, even after Christianity had spread across Europe and mankind had abandoned the pagan gods. Christian clergy were wise enough not to discard the old pagan customs, but adapted them to the new religion, simply giving the ceremonies, which were an established part of life, a Christian dimension, and the 'Birthday of the Unconquered Sun' became the 'Birthday of the Saviour'. Christmas became a mixture of solemn worship and festivity.

Over the 500 years when Vikings scourged Scotland's coasts they brought their own mid-winter festival with them and it was they who gave it the name by which it is still known — *Yule*. Norsemen had as hearty an appetite for enjoyment as for war and their Yule celebration lasted 24 days crammed with overindulgence which started off with a

prodigious feast on the eve of Yule. That night they consumed vast quantities of food and liquor, honouring their sun goddess, Freya, in their toasts, before they went out into the winter night to light a great bonfire in the goddess's honour. To this day, fire and light form a part of Yule celebrations in areas of Scotland as far apart as Biggar and Shetland. In Scandinavia, too, candles and fires illuminate Yule.

When William of Normandy conquered England in 1066 the English Princess Margaret had to flee, but was shipwrecked on the Scottish coast. The Scottish King, Malcolm Canmore, offered her refuge and later married her and, as his queen, Margaret laid a gentle Christian hand on her new country. As a result Christmas Day became the focus of Scotland's Yule celebration, and so it remained throughout the Middle Ages. On the eve of Christmas and on Christmas Day solemn masses were said and feasting and festivity followed.

Ancient superstitions and rites still clung to the Christian celebration. Houses continued to be decorated with mistletoe and evergreens; a festive porridge, derived from an old fertility rite, was eaten, and fires were lit. Feasting and dancing went on for days.

Gradually new influences began to shape these Christmas festivities, as the Middle Ages strengthened the links between Scotland and European countries as far apart as Scandinavia and Spain, or Holland and Russia. Above all France set her stamp on the festival to give us customs and foods which today remain an inseparable part of the New Year festivities.

By then the Yule festival had developed into the Twelve Days of Christmas, which became known in Scotland as the Daft Days, a direct translation of the French *Fête de Fous*. Society, from richest to poorest, celebrated the Daft Days. The royal court gave a lead; a Lord or Abbot of Misrule was appointed to organise the feasting and entertainment during the Daft Days, which included a great feast washed down with hot spiced wine served from a 'tappit hen', a large bowl with a spigot. Troupes of guisers entertained with plays, mumming, games, card-playing and dancing. The celebration ended with more wine and the singing of a Christmas hymn.

While the nobles and merchants were busy with their feasts and other festivities, their servants and the tradesmen and apprentices in the burghs enjoyed their own celebration. They were each given a handsel (or present) of a small amount of money, which they went out to spend in the alehouses or shops. Since this was probably the only holiday they had in the entire year, apart perhaps from a Fair Day, Christmas was looked forward to for weeks ahead and looked back on with joy by the entire community.

As you would expect the Church was at the centre of the Christmas festival, but not just as a place where masses were said to mark Christ's birth. Inside churches, even at the the the altar rail, much of the licenciousness of the old Saturnalia continued to be enacted. Processions and mock masses, led by the Abbot of Narent or Misrule, were little short of sacrilege; priests and monks stood back and allowed themselves and their services to be parodied and mocked.

People dressed up as donkeys and dragons cavorted and danced through the church, chasing a boy disguised as Sabina, daughter of the King of Egypt. It was a huge unseemly melee in which townsmen were dressed as bears, wolves and other wild animals. Robin Hood and Little John led outlaw bands, and the whole everyday world was turned upside down with men disguised as women and women as men; old men pretended to be children while the young walked on mock crutches and acted aged. At the very least, people turned their coats inside out and blackened their faces to join in the fun.

On St Nicholas's Day, 6 December, the children's festival began, when a Boy Bishop was appointed to rule until Childermas or the Feast of the Innocents, 28 December, the day which marked Herod's massacre of the firstborn babies.

Throughout this time churches were turned into vast, throbbing playgrounds, where anyone was free to make fun of the Church and temporal rulers, and naturally the horseplay became boisterous and vulgar. Profane songs were sung and unholy masses were said, but no one stopped it. This impiety was not confined to Scotland, but went on in other parts of Europe as well.

Even the monarch was not immune from being satirised; in 1540 King James V watched as Sir David Lyndsay's play, *Ane Pleasant Satyre of the Thrie Estatis*, mocked the corruption in his government and the Church. These were remarkably tolerant times.

Right up to the moment the Reformers took over, Christmas continued to be the celebrated in this way and was the highlight of life in Scotland at mid-winter. For nobility and common folk alike the sacred and profane elbowed each other to rule for a few brief days, which were the only breath of freedom they knew in their lives. It may not always have been very edifying, without doubt it was profane, but to all sections of society it was an essential part of life, not to be missed.

The fun ended with Twelfth Night which was called *Uphalieday* in Scotland, a day which was always a very special festival at the royal court, with guisers, dancing, plays and a night of endless revelry and merriment — all the enjoyments of Yule brought together into one great

night of daftness to round off the Daft Days.

To choose a 'king' and 'queen' to preside over the Uphalieday festivities a rich cake was baked — the ancestor of our traditional Black Bun — and a bean and a pea were concealed in it. The man who discovered the bean and the woman who found the pea were declared King and Queen of the Bean for the evening.

After Mary Queen of Scots returned to Scotland from France, she 'abdicated' at the Twelfth Night festivities in favour of two of her Marys — Mary Beaton and Mary Fleming — who were chosen as Queens of the Bean. In 1563 Mary herself helped to dress Mary Fleming in her own royal robes and jewels. The fun was so fast and furious that the English ambassador in Edinburgh was stunned by the extravagance of it.

'My pen staggereth,' he wrote to the Earl of Leicester. 'The Queen of the Bean was that day in a gown of cloth of silver, her head, her neck, her shoulders, the rest of her whole body, so beset with stones, that more in our whole jewel house were not to be found.'

With the coming of the Reformation Scotland lost both its Christmas and Uphalieday carnivals. Only Black Bun survives as a reminder of the cake which held the secret of who would rule on the last night of the twelve Daft Days.

The Kirk's Alarm

*'It was intimat that the people keip not
Yule bot work their ordinarie work under
all highest censour of the Session.'*

Elgin Kirk Session records, 24 December 1648

In the sixteenth century the Reformation overturned more than the nation's religious beliefs. It brought a sterner, narrower regimen for living, in which the keeping of Christmas in the old idolatrous way had no place. Records of the momentous century and a half between 1520 and 1680 trace the change:

1528 In Aberdeen, Reformers John and Robert Arthur are summoned to appear in the Church of St Nicholas 'with bare feet and wax candles in their hands, and publicly to beg the pardon of the Provost and Magistrates for having troubled the Lords of Bon Accord by preventing dancing.'

1540 In Linlithgow, on the Feast of Epiphany, Sir David Lindsay's play *Ane Pleasant Satyre of the Thrie Estaitis*, a fierce attack on the Church, is performed before the King and Queen.

1547 At Borthwick Castle the representative of the Primate of St Andrews arrives with letters of excommunication against the Lord or Abbot of Misrule, only to find the people celebrating with an unseemly procession, led by the Abbot of Unreason. The Primate's official is beaten, ducked in the mill dam, and made to eat the letter of excommunication after it had been soaked in wine.

1555 Parliament passes an Act banning the Abbot of Unreason. Punishment for 'Provost, Bailies, Counsell and Community' who disobey are to 'lose their freedom for a space of five years'.

1574 Aberdeen Kirk Session summons people before them for 'playing, dancing and singing filthy carols on Yule Day'.

1581 Perth Kirk Session acts against idolatrous and superstitious pastimes, especially against the 'Sanct Ober's Play'.

1582 In Glasgow five people are charged with 'observing the day called Yule'.

1597 A St Andrews baker is reported for 'keeping *Zwil* (Yule) in his house, the same being full of lichtis and mony in cumpany, hymself, cryit with lowd voice, superstitiously, "Zwill, Zwill, Zwill".'

1598 Elgin Kirk Session, 30 December: 'George Kay accusit of dansing and guysing in the night on Monday last. He confesses he had his sister's coat upon him and the rest that were with him had claythis dammaskit about thame and thair faces blaikit, and they had a lad play and upon banis and bells with them. Arche Hay had a faise about his loynes and kerche about his face. Ordained to make repentance two Sundays bairfut and bairleggit.'

1599 Elgin Kirk Session: 'Anent the Chanonrie Kirk. All prophane pastyme inhibited to be usitt be any persones ather within the burgh or college and specallie futballing through the toun, snaw balling, singing of carrellis or uther prophane sangis, guysing, pyping, violing, and dansing and specallie all thir above spect. forbidden in the Chanonrie Kirk or Kirk yard thairoff (except futball). All women and lassis forbiddin to haunt or resort thair under the paynis of publict repentans, at the leist during this tyme quhilk is superstitiouslie keipitt fra the xxv day of December to the last day of Januar nixt thairefter.'

1600 The King refuses to forego Christmas and it is 'solemnlie keepit' with merriment and cannonfire from Edinburgh Castle.

1605 Aberdeen revellers are brought before the Kirk Session for going through the city 'maskit and dancing'.

1617 James VI decrees that Christmas should be observed in Scotland as it is in England, but the Scots denounce this as a return to the ancient Saturnalia.

1630 Elgin Kirk Session: 'Alexander Innes purgit himselff be his oath that he was frie of any gyseing about Yule. William Sutherland confessit himselff to have been gyseing in womenis habits about the Yule tyme. To pay 40s. Alexander Innes, litster, confessit gyseing with a false beard at Yule tyme. Ordant to pay 20s.'

1638 General Assembly calls for abolition of Yule holiday.

1642 As Yule falls on a Sunday, Aberdeen ministers preach against 'all merriness, play and pastime.' On Monday the bellringer goes through the town ordering shops to open and men to go to work. Students seize the bell and the townsfolk celebrate as usual.

1645 General Assembly forbids schoolmasters from giving pupils a holiday at Christmas.

1649 General Assembly decides that since the people cannot hold Christmas without retaining Yule practice, both should be abolished.

1651 Cromwell, who is occupying Edinburgh, bans Christmas, but still the people celebrate until their lanterns turn the capital's night into day.

1659 Elgin: Rev Murdo McKenzie scours the town to prevent the Popish observance' of eating goose.

1659 South Ronaldsay, Orkney: 'James Scarty being found to be ane ordinar Sabath breaker, and to have upon New Yier even, under night, come to the minister his houss, and thair sung wantone and prophaine songs in contempt of the minister, and prophaned God's name, he is ordained to mak his publict repentance in sackcloth before the pulpit, and pay his penalty.'

1660 Elgin: 'The ministers did inquire at the elders of the cariage of the people relating to the supersitious tymes. They declared they saw nothing but guid order.'

1680 Edinburgh students indulge in revels on Christmas Day and end up burning an effigy.

Christmas was showing remarkable resilience in spite of the Kirk's disapproval, but slowly it had turned from a religious to a secular festival. About this time it became known as Hogmanay.

Rite and Day

Wind from the West, fishe and breas;
Wind from the North, cold and flaying;
Wind from the East, snow on the hills;
Wind from the South, fruit on the trees.

Highland Hogmanay rhyme, quoted by
F Marian McNeill in The Silver Bough

In spite of the Kirk's witch-hunting and demands for barefoot penance the Christmas festival did not die. It simply went underground. Instead of being celebrated joyfully, noisily and communally in public, it became centred on the home, limited to close and trusted family and friends. In time, in order to placate the Kirk, it was moved to the latter end of the Daft Days, which happened to coincide with the start of the New Year.

By the end of the seventeenth century the Scottish mid-winter festival emerged into the open again with a new name, *Hogmanay*, and marking the start of the new year — a reason with which neither Kirk or strait-laced Puritan could quarrel. Underneath it remained the same old celebration with all the rites and trappings of the ancient mid-winter junket.

Rituals had been adapted and changed out of all recognition until it was often impossible to trace their origins. People no longer believed in the magic powers behind them, but they still carried the rites out to the letter.

FIRST-FOOTING

At the heart of Hogmanay is the first-footing ceremony. The first person to cross the threshold brings all the luck, good or ill, for the year ahead, so he has to fulfil the strict criteria laid down by tradition.

The first-foot has to be male, tall, dark-haired, but not a doctor, minister or grave-digger. Thieves and fey folk are also shunned. He must be healthy and without deformity or handicap, although an accidental disability is acceptable. A limp, deformed foot, blindness or deafness are all reckoned to bring ill luck, as also are flat feet or eyebrows which meet in the middle.

Physical perfection is not sufficient: the first-foot should be honest, generous, good tempered and liked by all. And he must not carry a knife or other sharp tool. No wonder the first-foot is awaited with a mixture of excitement and apprehension. The wrong first-foot across the doorstep could spoil everything and be blamed for anything that goes wrong during the succeeding twelve months. To avoid this danger, families often arrange for their house to have a first-footer who meets all the conditions that custom demands.

What if by ill chance a poor, wee, ill-looking bauchle arrives at the door? The Scots' sense of hospitality would not allow him to be turned away, but tradition allows for the situation to be saved by fixing a cross made of rowan twigs above the door as a precaution. If the unlucky first-foot actually enters, the host must rush forward and speak before he or she can utter a word, bringing in the name of the Supreme Being three times. Roman Catholics should cross themselves as they speak to the unwelcome first-foot. Another simpler remedy is to throw salt into the fire the moment the first-foot is seen, to burn a piece of straw up the chimney, or even to take an ember from the fire and put it in a bowl of water next morning. One way or another ill fortune can be averted!

The most important rule for the first-footer is that he should not arrive empty handed. There are no set rules about what he should bring, other than a bottle from which to pour a drink for his host. A piece of coal or peat and cake are traditional, or even a sheaf of corn in country districts and around Dundee the first-foot always used to arrive with a be-ribboned red herring! However, any gift is acceptable from a box of chocolates to something useful for the house.

Without a word the first-footer walks to the fire and places the coal on it, then pours a drink from his bottle and hands it to his host. 'A guid

new year to ane an a',' is the most common toast as the head of the house drains the glass. Then the host pours a dram for the first-foot and the fun can begin. The first-footer can claim a kiss from every woman in the house and more toasts and songs follow. By this time more revellers will have arrived and all will be given drinks and food — the traditional shortbread, cake and Black Bun.

PREPARING THE HOUSE

In the old days it was considered bad luck for the house to be unclean or untidy at midnight on Hogmanay. As a result housewives spent days scrubbing and polishing until the place shone and in the dying minutes of the year they put out the last of the dirt and the ashes from the fire. The byre, also, was cleansed and purified with juniper fumes.

Walls, floors and doorposts were sprinkled with water specially brought from the well, or even with urine, and dried juniper was burned to cleanse the interior of the house. Rowan was placed above the door for luck, holly to keep the fairies out, mistletoe to prevent illness and hazel and yew because of their magic powers to protect all who resided in the house. After the burning of the juniper, doors were opened to allow fresh air to drive out the fumes and only then was the house considered ready for the New Year.

After the stroke of midnight nothing could be taken from the house until something had been brought in. Old-fashioned folk would not give or lend anything on the first day of the year, not from miserliness, but because they considered they would be handing away their good luck. Even the sweepings from the floor were not thrown out on New Year's Day.

FIRE AND WATER RITUALS

As might be expected in a festival whose origins lay in propitiating the sun god, those elements essential to life — fire and water — played an important part in the New Year rites. Bonfires were lit in many places and elaborate water rites were observed, principally the fetching of the first water on New Year's morning which was known as the 'Creaming of the Well'. The first person to draw water was lucky, so there was always competition to be there ahead of the rest of the village that day.

Fire was important, so it was considered unlucky to give anyone so much as a light to take ashes out of the house on New Year's Day. The fireplaces told much. If a peat or live coal rolled away, someone would depart during the year; if the fire burned brightly prosperity would follow, but if it just smouldered a year of adversity lay ahead. On New Year's morning the fire was raked and the ashes examined carefully for omens of death and ill fortune.

BIRTH, MARRIAGE AND DEATH

Both death and birth could be found in the shape the ashes took when the fire was raked — the shape of a footprint pointing out the door presaged a death during the year; a print pointing inwards predicted an addition to the family. Birth, marriage and death were all subject to omens — mostly terrible!

In Aberdeenshire a new-born baby which gave three 'greets' at New Year was considered to be sure to live to a ripe old age. In places as far apart as Lewis and Perthshire it was considered unlucky to marry during the first twelve days of the year. In Galloway, however, January was a noted time for weddings. Convenience met superstition head-on in this, and the Yule holiday became a popular time for working people to marry; after all it was the only day many of them had free in the entire year.

It brought the worst of ill luck to allow a dead body to lie in the house over Hogmanay, so if someone died during the last days of December, burial was hastily arranged before the year's end. An Ayrshire man was quoted as saying of his wife, 'She was removed from mine to Abraham's bosom on Christmas Day, and buried on Hogmanay; for it was thought uncanny to have a dead corpse in the house on the New Year's Day.'

Boys beat one another with branches of holly until they drew blood in the belief that they would live a year for every drop shed — a painful way to ensure longevity!

WEATHER SIGNS

Throughout Hogmanay and New Year's Day the sky was watched for signs, which would indicate the weather that could be expected for the harvest in the year ahead. Every breath of wind, each cloud's path, was followed and they called the cloud which passed over at gloaming on Hogmanay the Candlemas Bull. Its shape and position determined the weather for the year. The weather on Hogmanay and through the first eleven days of January were also believed to predict what would lie ahead month by month for the rest of the year.

NEW YEAR'S DAY OMENS

As many omens could be drawn from New Year's Day as from Hogmanay. As if there had not been enough signs of good luck or bad (and an amazing number of things can bode ill for the house on that day!) it started from the moment of waking: to set eyes on someone of the opposite sex was a good omen, but in Sutherland it was considered unlucky to see a woman first on New Year's morning. This must have presented problems for Sutherland husbands! To see a group of people presaged a death of someone in the family, and even an animal lying down or with its hindquarters turned towards the viewer boded ill. Flights of birds could herald bad luck also.

HARVEST SIGNS

At New Year's dawn a red sky — which countrymen saw as a bad sign on any day of the year — also boded ill. Country and coast folk watched the way the wind blew because it told them what kind of crops to expect or how successful their fishing would be.

In the Moray Firth fishing villages superstition was strong. There sea water was carried into houses and sprinkled on the fire and seawood was placed over the door and at each corner of the house. Fishermen competed to be the first to shoot their lines on New Year's morning and the first to 'draw blood' could expect good luck that year. If the weather was too wild for the boats to put to sea, then the fishermen would take their guns and shoot an animal. The important thing was to shed blood.

Omens were everywhere at New Year — in the fire, in what jobs could or could not be done in the house, in how work was begun. With so many possibilities of bringing bad luck, it is surprising anyone rose to face the first day of the year.

The Lowland New Year — Hogmanay

An Open Door and a Het Pint

Wi' muckle (1) glee, but little din,
At doors the lassies sentries keep,
To let the first-fit in.
Nae auld, camshauchled (2) warlock loon (3),
Nor black, wanchancie carlin (4)
Sall cross ae threshold o' the toun
Till ilk lass gets her darlin' person
To kiss that nicht.

Poems of the Rev James Nicol, 1805

It was industrialisation and the expansion of towns during the nineteenth century that really made Hogmanay the common man's festival, for it marked the only break in the long winter for working men and women, so they were determined to make the most of it. People worked together, lived closely packed into towns, and spent their little leisure time together, so it was natural for them to welcome in the New Year communally.

It became the custom to gather at a convenient central point on Hogmanay, usually the square, the mercat cross, or outside the church. The town clock was popular because this was one place at which one

(1) much; (2) deformed; (3) lad; (4) unlucky fellow

could be sure to know the exact stroke of midnight.

Every town grew to have its own Hogmanay rendezvous. In Edinburgh the Tron Kirk, half way down the Royal Mile, became the place at which to welcome in the New Year. Glasgow folk saw it in at Glasgow Cross, where the Gallowgate and Trongate meet. In recent years a more formal assembly has been organised, complete with official invitations, at George Square, which is the heart of today's Glasgow. Other towns had their own Hogmanay trysting places:

Aberdeen — The foot of Union Street outside the Town House

Alexandria, Vale of Leven — The fountain where the roads from Dumbarton, Bonhill and Balloch meet

Ayr — The Cross outside the Town Buildings at the bottom of the High Street

Arbroath — The Steeple, Kirk Square, in the middle of the High Street (once site of the town's well)

Airdrie — The old Cross (now gone as a result of redevelopment)

Dumfries — The Midsteeple

Dundee — City Square

Dunfermline — The Town Cross, High Street

Elgin — The old mercat cross at the end of the town

Falkirk — The Steeple, High Street

Forres — The mercat cross at the Tolbooth

Galashiels — The Clock Tower by the War Memorial

Jedburgh — The Cross

Kelso — Town Hall in The Square

Kilmarnock — The Cross (now redeveloped)

Montrose — Outside the Town House and the Steeple, where the mercat cross once stood

Paisley — The Town Hall

Perth — The Cross, at junction of High Street and Skinnergate (now marked on road outside

St John's Centre)

Stirling — The Steeple at the top of King Street

Stranraer — The Cross

The scene was the same everywhere: the crowd swelled during the minutes leading up to midnight, almost everyone carrying a bottle and all with a muted air of expectancy. As the clock's hands moved towards the magic moment, the crowd fell silent, counting the seconds, holding their breath and waiting for the first stroke of twelve. That lit the touch-paper. The street, so still one moment, exploded into cheering, singing and joyous movement. Hands were shaken, women were kissed, and bottles were offered all round. Spontaneously, all broke into a chorus of *Auld Lang Syne*, with church bells as background to the bedlam.

In seaports ships' sirens blared and in mining towns and villages the pit horns blew. In the country many farmers fired a shotgun in the air to give the *coup de grace* to the old year.

At urban meeting places the circle widened as the crowd broke up into small groups of friends preparing to set out to first-foot relatives and friends. By one o'clock the place was almost deserted.

The great Hogmanay drink in the old days was Het Pint, a brew of ale mulled with nutmeg and whisky. This was carried, steaming hot, in a copper kettle and poured into cups which were offered to everybody the first-footer met on his travels. The Het Pint has vanished in favour of the whisky bottle, but the name still survives in Lanark where they carry out the Ceremony of the Het Pint each New Year's morning. This tradition, perpetuating an older Ne'erday tradition at which old people of the town were given a pint of ale, takes place outside the Local District Council offices, when elderly residents of the town can claim one pound and a glass of beer.

For many families it took weeks of hard saving and overtime work to gather together enough to pay for the New Year dram. Savings clubs were, and still are, a popular way of saving up to buy in the festive season drink. Up to half a century ago, when men worked together in large groups in heavy industry, nearly every factory had one or more savings groups within it. The night of the shareout was a great occasion at which whisky and beer flowed almost as freely as on the last night of the year — a Hogmanay preview during which a largish portion of a man's savings could be spent. In earlier times groups of workers often pooled their money to buy a cask of whisky, which was solemnly divided out to be carried home in bottles or cans ready for Hogmanay. The temptation was sometimes too great and on occasions the bottle arrived home empty and its guardian full!

The source of the whisky in those days was dubious to say the least. James Barr, writing of the Vale of Leven in Dumbartonshire long ago, describes one such distillation, supplied by a well known local moonshine expert. When the cask was broached, the whisky had a milky appearance, which the supplier explained away as emanating from 'a new London barm' from which it was made. The distillation was tasted suspiciously, but eventually pronounced drinkable and shared out. There have been occasions when illegally distilled spirits have had less happy results, sometimes even fatal.

Menfolk took care of provision of the drink, while women and children were responsible for the food. The poor, who could not afford a feast of their own, had a way of ensuring that they would have plenty. On Hogmanay young people went guising from door to door, dressed up often in clothes of the opposite sex and wearing a large apron folded to form a sack in which to collect as they went round the houses. They chanted:

> *Rise up, guid wife, an' shake your feathers,*
> *Dinna think that we are beggars:*
> *We are bairns come out to play,*
> *Get up and gie's our Hogmanay!*

Others made a simpler, more direct plea:

> *My feet's cauld, my shoon's done,*
> *Gie's my cakes, and let me rin.*

Around Newburgh in Fife they had another chant which (in the words of a local writer) set 'both music and grammar at defiance':

> *Round the midden I whuppit a geese;*
> *I'll sing nae mair till I get a bit piece(1).*

Every household gave something — oatcakes, Black Bun, shortbread or drinks. If the guisers were turned away empty-handed, they had another chant which left the housewife in no doubt about what they felt. It ended:

(1) Food/snack

Gin ye dinna gie's our Hogmanay,
We'll dunner a'yer doors (2) the day.

As well as blacking faces and wearing women's clothes, the guisers used straw to make helmets and ropes which they decorated with ribbons. In this disguise they went round the doors, accompanied by a fiddler, dancing and performing an ancient play and collecting a reward of food or money.

The guisers' play was called *The Goloshan*, a form of the Christmas mummers' play, which originated as a mediaeval court masque. *The Goloshan*, said to be derived from Galgacus, the ancient Caledonian leader who fought against the Romans, was originally performed by a group of men dressed in white and called the White Boys of Yule and one in black representing Beelzebub. Each district had its own version of the play, which survived in various parts, from Shetland to Galloway, into quite recent times. Although it was often laced with snatches of Shakespeare's *Macbeth*, Home's *Douglas* and Allan Ramsay's *Gentle Shepherd*, *The Goloshan* became a kind of saints' play in keeping with the season, starting with the 'Rise up gudewife and shake your feathers' rhyme, then turning into a confrontation between Galgacus and the King of Macedon. There was a splendid swordfight in which the Caledonian chief was slain and then brought back to life, so all ended well. At the end a bag is passed round and money collected.

The guisers, often accompanied by a fiddler and a singer, were looked forward to eagerly by those they visited, people who knew nothing but drudgery and poverty throughout the rest of the year.

Guising nowadays takes place only at Hallowe'en in Scotland and the *Goloshan* play has disappeared. A 71-year-old correspondent from Jedburgh told me of hearing of it from her parents who had taken part in it, although by her own childhood it had degenerated into nothing more than going round the farmhouses on Hogmanay and receiving a bag of 'goodies' from the farmer's wife. Now even that has vanished.

With guisers, songs, saints and sinners, and mummers' plays, Hogmanay and Christmas remained close to one another, yet they never quite united to form a single celebration.

Pre-Christian rites of fire and light have lingered on too, although

(2) thump on your doors

there are fewer of these today than there once were. Up to the first quarter of the twentieth century bonfires were commonplace, just as they had been throughout Viking times. Towns as far apart as Newton Stewart, Dingwall, Comrie and Campbeltown all had their Hogmanay fires and in communities which depended on the sea there was a tradition of burning a boat. Up to the turn of the nineteenth century the local newspaper in Stranraer carried a report most years about the burning of a boat by fisherfolk who lived in the seafront houses in old Market Street. Burning a boat at Hogmanay was also common throughout the North East and was even the custom on the far northern coast at Bettyhill in Sutherland.

A correspondent who grew up in Invergordon in the 1930s described the Hogmanay bonfire there:

> *Sometime in early December a pole was erected on a small plot of land just east of the town and by the seashore. During the following weeks the local men, many of whom were unemployed at that time, cut whins, collected old tyres, oil, wood and gradually built a bonfire round the pole. On New Year's Eve the Boy Scout pipe band paraded up and down the High Street and ended playing round the fountain which was situated in the centre of High Street at the junction of Castle and King Streets. At midnight the fire was lit and I recall a bottle of whisky was passed round all those who had built the bonfire. As far as I recall, the fire signified the burning of all that was bad in the past year and to start the new year with a 'clean slate'.*

Dwindling rural communities and the outbreak of the Second World War in 1939 brought most of the old fire ceremonies to an end, but a few still survive. The most spectacular of these are at Biggar, Comrie, Stonehaven and Burghead; the first three on Hogmanay and the last on New Year's Eve by the pre-1752 Old Style calendar. In that year the government decided to harmonise Britain's calendar with the continental Gregorian one, which required eleven days to be dropped from our calendar. Consequently it was decreed that eleven days of September that year would simply be wiped out — obliterated from people's lives! Naturally the people were angry and demanded to be given back the days which had been stolen from them.

Many continued to follow the old calendar and when Hogmanay came round they simply ignored it and waited until 11 January to celebrate. This date became known as Old New Year or Auld New Year.

Since time immemorial there has always been a bonfire in the High Street of Biggar on Hogmanay. It is lit at about half past nine in the evening, when the street becomes so crowded that traffic eventually just gives up trying to pass through. The bonfire is not formally organised — it just happens! Police and fire authorities appear to be the only people in the town who are against it. However, it thrives on opposition and is lit each year with great ceremony. Even during the Second World War, when bonfires were banned, the tradition was kept 'alight' by a woman resident of the town who went out each Hogmanay and struck a match at the spot where the fire was normally lit. The bonfire has been

filmed at various times and once was even lit in August to allow the custom to be filmed for television. On that night a new doctor who had just arrived in Biggar was called to attend an old lady who lay at death's door. When he went in, he remarked, 'Do you know there's a funny thing going on in the town: there's a large bonfire in the main street.'

'My God!' she replied, 'is it that time of the year already?'

At Comrie they call their fire observance the Flambeaux Ceremony; it serves a double purpose of a beating of the bounds and an ancient rite of chasing away evil spirits. The flambeaux used are small birch trees with a two-foot length at the end swathed in combustible material, bound with wire and soaked in paraffin. On Hogmanay these are lit on the stroke of midnight and are carried ceremonially to each part of the town.

The flambeaux carriers are preceded by a piper and followed by crowds of people in fancy dress. Decorated floats also take part in the procession, which finishes at the town square where the flambeaux are thrown together to make a bonfire.

At Stonehaven they welcome the New Year and ward off evil spirits in spectacular fashion with a fireball swinging ritual whose beginning is lost in time — or perhaps it isn't! No one knows the real origin of this unique ceremony, but it is thought to be a modern adaptation of a more ancient rite. Certainly since before the 1914-18 war great balls of fire have swung down the town's High Street as each old year dies away and the new one begins.

When the old town clock strikes midnight on Hogmanay and the bells ring in the new year, the town's pipe band swings along from the town cross by the old steeple to the cannon at the far end of the High Street. Behind them follow as many as 40 men and women birling flaming balls round their heads like fiery flags, miraculously missing the crowds who pack the street to watch.

During the preceding week, the young men of the town make balls out of any combustible material, well packed to burn as long as possible and wrapped in sacking, then bound in wire netting. A foot or two of rope enables the ignited ball to be swung round the head, shooting its flames and light into the Hogmanay darkness. Describing the scene in the 1960s, F A S Cairn wrote:

The pavements were more than packed, and the crown of the causey was left to the fireball swingers. The swinging balls were an assurance that the swingers would not be subjected to crowding. The crow-stepped gables and the eighteenth century frontages were ruddy in the glare, as they had been when Butcher Cumberland made a bonfire — in the same street — of the pews from a nearby chapel whose congregation had Jacobite sympathies.

The assembled crowds thought not of the past, but of the future, as they pushed their way along, shaking hands with everybody they met in an orgy of goodwill.

Considering that some of the swingers had been 'celebrating' earlier in the evening, the number of accidents was very few.

I have seen a tipsy swinger fall over his flaming ball, pick himself up and continue his march. The worst I ever heard of was that one spectator who had gone too far into the street had his back hair singed and all the comfort he got was to be told that it would save the expense of a haircut.

But the bell has stopped; the moving finger of Time has traced out another quarter of an hour, and the fireballs have burnt out. The rite of welcoming the returning sun by fire has duly been performed for another year, and the crowds skail to the serious business of first-footing.

First-footing brings Hogmanay out of the community back into the home, where many have always preferred to welcome the New Year. Stay-at-home families gather round the fire which is well stoked to ensure a good blaze at midnight in order to bring good luck throughout the coming year. Towards midnight a hush falls, and the man of the house opens the front and back doors to let the old year out and the new one in. On the stroke of midnight the whole family makes a great noise, banging tin trays, blowing whistles and shouting to drive out any bad spirits that might be lurking within the rooms.

The first-foot is now awaited, and he and other revellers will all be given drinks and cake (shortbread, cake and Black Bun). At some point 'Auld Lang Syne' must be sung — possibly it will be sung at several points! — and the first-footers move on.

In many houses the door used to stand open until well into the early hours of New Year's Day, for Hogmanay lasts as long as family and first-footers have stamina. Like old soldiers, Hogmanay never dies — it only fades away!

The Lowland New Year — New Year's Day

Into the Unknown Year

That merry day the year begins,
They bar the door on frosty win's
The nappy reeks wi' mantling ream(1),
An' sheds a heart-inspiring steam;
The luntan (2) pipe, an' sneeshin mill(3),
Are handed round wi' right guid will;
The cantie (4), auld folks, crackan crouse(5),
The young anes rantan thro' the house —
My heart has been sae fain(6) to see them,
That I for joy hae barket wi' them.

The Twa Dogs, Robert Burns

It is hard to believe it, but once upon a time there was keen competition to be first up on New Year's morning. In spite of the excesses of the night before, New Year's Day was — and still is — a busy one for many people. While one half of the population sleeps off the overindulgence of the night before, the other half continues the festivities with family gatherings.

It was not always like this: up to the start of the Second World War in 1939, New Year's Day was another working day for most, although

(1) froth; (2) smoking; (3) snuff mill; (4) cheerful; (5) chatting merrily; (6) anxious

some factories and shipyards did close down. At Ardrossan the shipyard holiday actually extended to ten days in 1922, but that was probably due to lack of orders as much as Ne'erday goodwill.

On farms the year traditionally began with a visit to the stable and byre to give the animals an extra feed, usually a sheaf of corn for the horses and cows. In his poem *The Auld Farmer's New Year Morning Salutation*, Robert Burns makes this visit a sentimental moment of reminiscence between the ageing farmer and his old mare, Maggie. It is a typical Scottish Ne'erday response to the passing years and equally typical of Burns's genius for fathoming the Scottish character.

> *A Guid New Year I wish thee, Maggie!*
> *Hae, there's a ripp(1) to thy auld baggie*
> *Tho tho's howe-backit(2) now, an knaggie (3),*
> *I've seen the day*
> *Thou could hae gaen like onie staggie,*
> *Out owre the lay (4).*

Farmworkers' families were given gifts of food and the farmers' wives put out food for the wild birds on New Year's Day. A special breakfast followed at which friends and neighbours were welcome to drop in. There was a dram on the table for all who wanted one and in the North East everybody was served sowans, a thin gruel made from the fermented inner husks of oats. Sowans was sweetened, usually with honey or black treacle, laced with whisky to turn it into a rich, creamy, heady mixture. Sowans and Yule were inseparable in the north, while Yule Brose containing meat was more common in the Lowlands.

The sowans was sometimes dished out in small bowls with charms hidden in them — a coin to denote wealth, a ring for marriage and a button to prophesy poor marriage prospects. The gruel was smeared on doors for good luck, so many a houseproud housewife must have felt the mess it left countered a lot of the good fortune!

There was an upside to all this supping of sowans and clarting it on folks' doors and windows. Some authorities claim it had sexual qualities and, because it resembled human sperm, farmlads teased young women by telling them, 'I'll be at you wi' my sowans.'

(1) sheaf of corn; (2) hump-backed; (3) bony; (4) lea

It was a good omen for the year ahead to start some job, although there was no need actually to do much work. It was sufficient for the womenfolk to cast on a piece of knitting.

The milkman and postman were out as usual on New Year's morning. In the 1930s our postie walked his round — four miles along the Low Road from Maybole in the morning, then up the lower slopes of Carrick Hill and back to Maybole by the High Road. The only difference from ordinary days was that the walk took longer on New Year's Day because he was invited in and given a dram at every house.

Ours was one of the few houses with a telephone in those days, and late on one New Year's Day, when there were several inches of snow lying on the ground, my father received a telephone call from the Postmaster in Maybole. Had we seen Postie Jock? Yes, he had delivered to us — late, but he had called and gone on his way. My father quickly rounded up neighbours who scoured the fields leading to the High Road, and in the gloaming they found, first the postbag, then Jock himself, drunk. They took him to the nearest house, thawed him out and sobered him up, then delivered the remaining mail and finally Jock himself back to the Post Office.

Jock was near retiring age, and it would have cost him his job and his pension if the story had got to the ears of the authorities, so a pact was made that nothing would be said of all this to the Postmaster. It was only long afterwards that we learnt that the Maybole Postmaster had soon heard all about Jock's escapade, but turned a blind eye so that he would not lose his pension.

On New Year's Day a lot of folk worked off the effects of all the feasting and drinking with sport and playing pranks on their elders and betters. They called this 'Devilment'. Right up to recent times it was common for young people to play tricks on their elders all through the Daft Days. Youths would collect all the carts in the neighbourhood on Hogmanay and haul them into the main street of the town where they caused an almighty blockage on New Year's morning. My grandfather used to tell how he and the other lads of the district set a piece of turf on the chimney of a house in the village which was unfortunate enough to be built into the side of a hill.

My mother had a story about how she and her best friend, Gracie, filled the whisky decanter with cold tea when her friend's father was entertaining some important friends on New Year's Day. Through the slightly ajar parlour door they watched as a generous dram was poured for each guest. First one sipped, then another, but they said nothing until their host lifted his glass.

'I doubt there's something wrong wi' the whisky,' one ventured. Gracie's father took a good gulp. 'God damn thae lassies,' he cried and summoned them, without a cross word, to fetch the right bottle.

The Devilment could be wild. At Roberton in the Borders it was the custom on the shortest day of the year for the oldest lads to bar the schoolmaster from the building. George Scott, who was present, described what followed:

> When Mr Amos arrived he found, as he expected, five lads in possession of the school; and the question was, how to get them out and regain possession. They had taken all precautions to make their position as strong as possible. The windows were covered with plaids, the door was barricaded with seats inside; in fact, all the means at their command were used to keep the besiegers at bay. On the other hand, those outside, led by Mr Amos, were just as determined to get in. I remember well there was snow on the ground on one occasion, and the master made us youngsters roll snowballs up against the door till he thought there was no chance of the lads getting out.
>
> He then went round to the back of the house, commenced to strip the thatch from the roof till he had made a hole large enough to allow himself to drop down on one of the desks. It was no easy task for him to do this, seeing he was lame and used a crutch; but he did it, and was soon followed by all the biggest boys, and the lads inside at once saw the game was up. There was a little window of four panes set in a frame opening with hinges, and Wull Scott opened this window, got his head and shoulders through and stuck.
>
> In trying to wriggle through, he managed to get the whole window and frame unloosed, and he ran up my father's yard with it sticking to his middle. Adam Pringle got up the chimney so far as to get his feet on the crooktree, where Mr Amos found him. The master at once ordered a fire to be kindled and very soon 'Yeddie' was glad to come down to avoid being suffocated.

Games took up a large part of New Year's Day and, being Scotland, ball games were great favourites — football, rugby or handball. Games were played with ferocity, little finesse and a lot of fun. In the Borders, where Rugby is part of their religion, the Ne'erday match was always a 'needle' encounter with local rivals pitching in, cheered on by the whole community. A cross-border soccer 'international' was often played, too; one year when Chirnside played host to a Northumberland Eleven, the home-team goalkeeper left his post, when his team was winning 2-0, to wish some friends a Happy New Year, but returned to find that the visitors were leading 2-3!

In the larger towns the New Year ball game developed into something very different. It became a spectator sport with a real needle match between local rival professional teams. This game was eagerly looked forward to by many who seldom attended a football match at any other time of the year. It was a great day out for city menfolk, giving them a chance to use up energy left over from Hogmanay and at the same time to nurse their hangover in good fresh air.

Around Kirkcaldy in Fife they had their own game called *Kyles*. This was a form of quoits whose name derived from the French game of *quilles* or quoits. Bets were laid and the game went furiously with cries of 'A penny she kyles'. In another part of Fife, at Wemyss, they had a game rather like French bowls, but called *Yettlings*, and believed to have been of Dutch or Flemish origin.

The farmers and country folk frequently gathered on the first morning of the year for a great shooting expedition, which was often more memorable for its conviviality than for its bag of game. Isabelle Shaw, who grew up at the Tibbie Shiels Inn in the Yarrow valley in the early years of the century, described the annual shoot, which was traditionally held on Hogmanay but merged into the New Year. She wrote:

> *On Old Year's Day usually, we had a gathering of local people both men and women in the forenoon and after light refreshments (or whiles not so light!) we all set forth — guns and beaters and dogs — and made for the hills to shoot white hares (not easily seen in snow) with many stops for wee sips and drams! There was a picnic lunch and then all returned home before 4 pm to count the spoils and have them hung.*

After baths and a change of clothes the ladies started preparations for the evening while the menfolk drank and cracked about the day's shoot and other things of interest until a good heavy meal was eaten before the celebrations began. We all gathered round the huge open peat fire in the Tibbie Shiels Inn — lamps glowing, fiddle music, so much chatter, and the table groaning with more food. On another table stood the half gallon bottle — filled for Hogmanay and it was only

put away once it was emptied. On the stroke of midnight by the old grandfather clock in the corner, we each lifted our glasses to herald the New Year, and then my mother, being the hostess, went to the door to greet the 'Young Year' and to say farewell to the 'old'. She would bow as she stood at the door — then along would come our first fit to be welcomed (only if *he was dark) and on the stroke of midnight he would run right round the house, carrying under his arm a white hare from the shoot, a lump of coal dangling from a string and of course a bottle of whisky. Usually he wore a shepherd's plaid. Then in he would come where all were greeted and wished a Happy New Year and the drinks were exchanged.*

Until the dawn broke there was much celebrating and songs and dancing. A huge pot of Irish Stew hung on the swee over the peat fire and plates of this were dished out at intervals. At daybreak one could see many auld local farmers wandering their staggering way through the snow, making for their respective homes. After much clearing up, everyone tried to have some rest because usually the same crowd would return to celebrate New Year's Day.

I remember it all well, the laughter, the smoke of many old men's pipes and the aftermath of so much celebration and my mother placing on the swee a hanging oven like a pot with a flat lid that was heaped with hot peats and the peats on the fire underneath. Inside the pot this time were thick gigot chops which had been steeped in porter all night and covered with chopped onions to cook. Barley scones or bread were served with this. Celebrations were still going on until the next dawn — and so began our New Year.

In the north-east folk took their fresh air in different fashion. Joseph Robertson, in *The Book of Bon Accord*, told of the procession in Aberdeen two centuries ago when servants and apprentices dressed up and marched, carrying banners and tools of their trades. 'The shoemakers,' he wrote, 'were headed by their patron, St Crispin (whom they advanced to the dignity of a crown) attended by a number of pages.' When the authorities tried to abolish the custom the apprentices rioted and some were thrown into jail. Their friends smashed the Town Hall windows and they were released.

In the north-east corner of Aberdeenshire, fisher folk of Buchan's wild Rathen coast had (and still have) their own processions, although they take their celebration more soberly. For the past 150 years villagers of Inverallochy, Cairnbulg and St Combs — all places with strong evangelical fervour — have joined in a series of Temperance Walks at Yule.

The walks began as a result of the regeneration of the villages after a disastrous period in the middle of the nineteenth Century. In those days, it was said, 'the men were combative and, under the influence of alcohol, desperate fights among them were a common occurence'. A terrible cholera epidemic brought this wild era to an end in 1847, and when the area began to grow again it was a very different community. Out of this the tradition of Temperance Walks was born.

The first of these, at Inverallochy, is held on Christmas Day, the second at Cairnbulg on New Year's Day and the third, at St Combs, on 2 January, although it used to be held on the fifth day of the month.

The walks are led by a flute band, for this corner of Buchan is as enthusiastic about flute music as it is about religion. The band is followed by the oldest man in the village and a female partner. More than 50 couples join in the walk, which sets out from Cairnbulg Gospel Hall at about 11 o'clock in the morning and takes in all three communities.

New Year's Day is traditionally a family time and the New Year's Day dinner brings members from more distant parts for a meal, very similar to the Christmas dinner which folk in other parts of Britain have enjoyed a week earlier.

The menu is dictated as much by what families can afford as by tradition. In the old days the main course might have been goose; today turkey, a roast of beef, or a steak pie is more usual.

In harder times it was difficult to spin the food out to fill everybody. A West Lothian man told me how every house there served steak pie that day and those who could not afford sufficient steak to go round the extended family added sausage meat cut in pieces so that it had the appearance of steak. They never used kidney to eke the meat out. These pies were often far too large to fit in the family oven, so they were taken to the local baker to be cooked in his bread oven. Never, never would any self-respecting West Lothian housewife serve a pie bought from a shop.

Another way of making the food go round was that favoured by my mother — she cunningly started the meal with a large plate of broth stiff with beans, peas, barley and vegetables which filled stomachs before the main course was on the table!. Ne'erday dinner traditionally ended with a Clootie Dumpling, a great, sweet fruit-filled pudding boiled in a cloth or cloot. More recently, trifle has been substituted for dumpling — a retrograde step, however delicious a Scottish trifle may be!

The New Year's Day menu rarely varied:

Scotch Broth
Steak Pie
Cabbage or Turnip (Swede) and Potatoes
Clootie Dumpling

It may seem strange that anyone had energy for games after such a meal, but games were played and more friends were visited during the rest of the day.

Nowadays, when the 1 and 2 of January are bank holidays, every town from Berwick to Lerwick is dead on New Year's Day and the day after. One might be forgiven for thinking that the whole of Scotland is 'sleeping off' its excesses of Hogmanay, but there is still a considerable degree of life and conviviality behind closed doors as families spend this time together, probably the only days they will share so closely in the whole of the year.

Perhaps this drawing together of the family is one of the most magical aspects of today's Scottish New Year.

Highlands and Islands New Year
Challuinn And Camanachd

Gu'm beannaicheadh Dia an t-fhardach,
Eadar Chlach, us chuaille, us chrann,
Eadar bhithe, bhliochd, us aodach,
Slainte dhaoin bhi daonnan ann.

God bless the dwelling,
Each stone and beam and stave,
All food and drink and clothing.
Good health to all in it.

Carmina Gadelica, Volume 1

Although first-footing is a key part of Oidhche na Challuinn, the Highland and Islands Hogmanay, the celebration has its own distinct character. For one thing even today Hogmanay remains much more a communal festival, particularly among remoter village and crofting communities. It must be said though that there, as elsewhere, it is changing.

Highlanders tell you Hallowe'en is as important to them as New Year, but they celebrate both, with Hallowe'en primarily for the children and New Year for the grown ups. There was always confusion in the Highlands as to when or how to celebrate the winter solstice festival; Roman Catholic parts prefer Christmas, Protestant areas choose Hogmanay, and the Northern Isles are still drawn to the Norse Yule. However, the last day of December has grown to be the principal festival throughout the north, and it is still enjoyed there with more gusto than almost anywhere in the Lowlands.

Lowlanders and Highlanders alike are agreed on that — especially those exiles from the north who now have their roots in the cities and towns of the south. In Glasgow exiles dream of *Challuinn* as they remember it back home. Needless to say, almost every man or woman to whom I have spoken has told me that *Challuinn* isn't what it used to be; yet Lowlanders who have spent a New Year in the Highlands are quick to say that Hogmanay in the north still retains a sense of magic which their own southern festival has lost.

Both are right. The changing lifestyle of the North may be eroding that communal spirit which has always marked out the Highland New Year and superstitions, customs and ancient rites may well be slipping from common usage, but they are taking a long time to die.

Guising, which was part of the Highland New Year just as it once was in the Lowlands, still clings on, although on a much smaller scale. Among Highland crofting communities and in the Western Isles guisers went out to collect the ingredients for their New Year's feast. The late John MacInnes, who lived in South Uist, told me about the old Hogmanay ritual there and on the other islands:

> *On Hogmanay night boys of school age and thereby got together and set out to visit all or most of the houses of the village. They had bags to hold gifts of bread, cakes, sweets and so on, which people gave them during the round. They were also armed with a* Caisean Challuinn, *which is basically the fat breast strip of a sheep rolled up in the rough round shape of a candle, which they lit after being admitted to the house. At Christmastime most families killed one of their sheep prior to the feast: the raw material for the* Caisean Challuinn *was obtained at this time.*
>
> *Before admission over the doorstep the boys had to recite or sing a song or poem or rune with historical or mystical meaning; some were short but others were long and rustic and told of battles long ago. A few of the boys would be experts in memorising and reciting these. The common Gaelic word was* duan — *a song, poem, or ode.*

All this is a corrupted form of a ceremony which Sir James Frazer, in *The Golden Bough*, traces back to prehistoric times not just in the islands of Scotland, but throughout Europe when a bull was led from door to door round the community before being sacrificed.

Dan Murray from Stornoway, told me that this guising ceremony takes place only in about three villages in the whole of the Western Isles today. 'Once *Oidhche na Challuinn* was the favourite festival among the youths of Lewis on Old Hogmanay. On that night boys would go

round the houses in the community, the leader draped in a calf's hide which was kept from year to year for the purpose. The others carried heavy sticks, usually their shinty sticks with a hide bag attached to the end of each. Led by the lad in the cowhide, they walked from house to house, making a great noise by beating their alms bags. At each house, they walked clockwise round the building, singing, banging their hides and making a great noise, then they sang a "port" or song at the door'. This went:

Ho ri vi o

A nochd oidhche nam bonnag,
Gabhaidh sinn an t-aran gun an t-im,
Gabhaidh sinn an t-im gun an t-aran,
Gabhaidh sinn a' chaise leatha fhein,
Is cuige a reisd a bhios sinn falamh?
Aon ni tha sinn ag aicheadh -
Suileagan a'bhuntata charraich,
Cumaidh iad naoidh trath gun cirigh,
An duine as treuna tha 'sa' bhaile

In English this means:

This is the night of the cakes,
We will take bread without butter,
We will take butter without bread,
We will take cheese all by itself.
So, how can we possibly lack food?
One thing alone do we refuse -
Small, wart-covered potatoes.
They'd keep the strongest man in the village
Nine times later abed.

On being admitted, the leading boy went up to the fire, which in the days of the old black houses burned in the middle of the room. He singed the end of his cowhide's tail, then walked round the room, allowing each of the inhabitants to sniff the smouldering hair, a rite which protected those who lived there from ill fortune during the coming year. In some places the smouldering tail was also passed three times round the head of the woman of the house. If the burning hair went out during this ceremony, it was an omen of bad luck for the household. In a more modern house the guisers would walk round a chair set in the middle of the room specially for the purpose.

When these rites had been completed, the visitors were given drink and some food to put into their sacks. The wife of the house was expected to hand over three cakes and the visitors gave her one of theirs in return. They then walked three times round the fire clockwise, singing a song, wishing good luck to all who lived there and to the animals too. If they were not received warmly or were refused gifts, the guisers walked round the fire in the opposite direction, marched out noisily and shook the dust of the house from their feet. Outside they intoned a curse and built a small cairn at the door.

In Lewis it was the custom for the boy carrying the calfskin to move round the fire, speaking his lines, while members of the family tried to hit him with the broom or some such weapon, and he had to shield himself from the blows with the calfskin. If nobody succeeded in striking him, he was given whatever food he asked for. In this way the young revellers collected bannocks, scones, cakes, jam and all the requisites for a feast. In the old days pennies were rarely given and whatever cash might be collected was quickly converted into eatables.

When the sack was full, the lads adjourned to the house of one of them and there prepared their feast. When all the food had been eaten the festivities continued with bagpipe-playing, dancing and storytelling — often tales of ghosts and fairies, for fairies were an important part of the Highland New Year. Nowadays the few youngsters who take part in guising around Lewis can earn a sizeable sum of money, so that nine guisers going round a community of say three hundred people can collect in the region of fifty pounds per boy or girl.

At midnight the Highland Hogmanay becomes the adults' festival just as it does elsewhere in Scotland. Guns are fired at croft doors to bid farewell to the old year and often men and women walk miles to first-foot, armed with their whisky bottle and food to ensure a year of happiness and plenty for every house in the community. The first-footers used to take specially baked thick oatcakes, but today shortbread is a more common first-footing gift.

In Inverness there were watchnight services and the townsfolk gathered to welcome the New Year at the Exchange, where the Old Steeple clock chimed the arrival of the New Year. The town band played and the crowd sang and wished friends and strangers alike a Happy New Year before setting out on their own first-footing expeditions. As in the south fewer people gather in the town centre nowadays and much of the Highland Capital's Hogmanay is focused on the private home or organised ceilidh rather than on meeting together as a community.

New Year's Day is sometimes called *Nollaig Bheag* or little Christmas, and this was a day of celebration. For entertainment the great Highland game of shinty, or *camanachd*, was a memorable event, when entire townships turned out to take part in or to watch a match between local rival teams. With pipers to urge the teams on, spectators were often tempted to join in until the game became a great free-for-all. A Dornoch minister in the last century recalled watching 'the whole male population, from grey-headed grandfather to the lightest-heeled stripling, turn out to the links, each with his club; and, from 11 o'clock in the forenoon, till it became dark they would keep at it, with all the keenness accompanied by shouts, with which their forefathers had wielded the claymore.' It was a most dangerous game for young and old, he added, and one can well believe the truth of that! A native of Iona has described the New Year's Day game there as golf, played by every man, woman and child on the island. There were no excuses, and everybody able to lift a golf club was compelled to take part.

Highland folk believed firmly in fairies — not the tinselly figure at the top of our Christmas tree today, but good and bad spirits who appeared and disappeared with alarming suddenness. They had to be humoured because they could cause much mischief and heartache when they chose. Hogmanay was their night, bringing a dimension of truth to the 'Hogmanay Trololay' rhyme, because that was the one night on which they were free to roam. Many tales were told of these wee folk, and of ghosts and witches as well at this season. It was easy to believe that people were enticed into a *sithean* or fairy hill on Hogmanay and returned home to find that a whole year had passed since they disappeared. Such tales proved that the rowan and the holly were more than an ancient superstition; they had a real part to play in the Highland Hogmanay.

Trolls played an important part in the mid-winter celebrations in the Northern Islands too. They left their homes in the heart of the earth and lived among humans for the period of Yule, playing tricks and wreaking every kind of havoc on humans, cattle, tools and crops; in human guise they joined in the merrymaking and seized any unfortunate person who did not take precautions to outwit them. At sunset crofters took two straws from a cornstack and laid them in the form of the cross at the entrance to the stackyard. They took a hair from each of their animals, plaited them and hung them above the byre door. Then a 'lowan tund' (a blazing peat) was carried through all the outbuildings to frighten the trolls away.

This was all part of the Viking festival of Yule as it was celebrated in Shetland. The festival lasted twenty-four days from Tulya's E'en until Up-Helly-Aa (meaning literally, the holiday has finished). This time was also known as the Merry Month, the equivalent of the southern Daft Days.

Shetlanders, being descendants of Vikings, love fire and light, so on New Year's Eve blazing tar barrels were dragged through Lerwick as townsfolk saw in the New Year in spectacular fashion. In other parts of Orkney and Shetland the year was welcomed much more staidly.

Once it was the custom in Orkney to gather on New Year's Eve at the various ancient standing stones which are to be found scattered around the isles. There revellers sang and danced the night away to welcome the New Year. Young people then went round the houses in the small hours of New Year's morning, singing a special New Year song. At each house they were invited in and sat down at a laden table to eat, before continuing to the next. It is hard to imagine how many suppers they ate on their travels, but the number must have been a substantial, for every household expected a visit and it gave offence if the food were to be refused. It was also considered a terrible slight for any family to be bypassed by the guisers.

On the western side of Shetland, in Walls and Sandness, young lads went guising on Hogmanay in groups of five to collect food for their New Year feast. The leader was called the 'gentleman' and it was his duty to sing their special song at each house, while another, known as the 'carrying horse' took charge of the bag in which gifts of food were placed. At Neuersmas (New Year's Day) the men and boys played football as long as daylight lasted.

At Kirkwall in Orkney, too, on New Year's Day the Uppies and Doonies Ba' Game was — and still is — the great event. With rules similar to the Eton Wall Game, the Kirkwall Ba' Game is played by lads born in the north end of the town, the Up-the-Gates, against those from the southern end, the Doon-the-Gates. The objective is to kick a leather ball filled with cork up to the 'head of the town' or down to the harbour.

The football game had few rules and needless to say it was interrupted frequently so that a dram could be passed round. Darkness brought the ball games to an end and then it was time for feasting, dancing, singing and storytelling to begin, but Northern Islanders had to be careful because trolls were excessively fond of dancing and would try to join in the revels in human disguise. When these festivities were in full swing in Shetland a gunshot was suddenly heard and the merriment stopped at once — the guisers had arrived. The head of the house went outside fired another shot in the air to signal that the guisers, known in Shetland as the *Skeklers* or *Grulicks*, were welcome. In the Grulicks came, disguised in white shirts covered with straw and with cloths over their faces to hide their identity.

Although work had to begin again on New Year's Day, even if only a token casting of a fishing line or setting out ingredients for baking, the Yule festival did not end then. Feasting and festivity continued right' through January until *Up-Helly-Aa*, on the eighteenth of the month, the last day of the twenty-four-day Yule holiday.

Up-Helly-Aa brought a mixture of happiness and fear which made every nerve tingle, for this was the trolls' last day of freedom and the time when they were at their most dangerous. Although the islanders danced the Yule festival away, they had to watch out for their own safety and for that of their children. People took care to carry amulets and not to go out alone on this day, and they made sure that their young people were sained and carefully watched over.

In Lerwick the Yule festival still culminates in a spectacular pageant in which a full-sized Viking galley is paraded through the streets, the Guiser Jarl standing in its prow and flanked by Viking warriors carrying blazing torches. Headed by bands, the galley progresses through the streets followed by guisers, townsfolk and Shetlanders who return to their native islands specially to be present at this ceremony. The galley is set alight at a public park in the town centre, after which the whole population continues with its revelries until morning.

This galley-burning ceremony has been dismissed as 'a queer travesty of old Norse customs', but Up-Helly-Aa has come to have deep significance for Shetlanders both at home on the islands and overseas. It is the event which reflects their origins and character, their 'national' festival.

By the time the Guiser Jarl's galley has burned itself out, Yule is over just as effectively as in the old days when Shetlanders opened their croft doors at midnight on Up-Helly-Aa night and raced out into the darkness to chase the last of the trolls back to their underworld home for another year, while young men disguised as Grulicks marched through the crofts with blazing torches.

Tomorrow is time for fishing, farmwork, spinning and weaving without a leavening of dancing or feasting: it really is Shetland's moment to return to old clothes and porridge. However, it is now 19 January and the days are beginning to lengthen. It is obvious to every eye that the sun is returning and Yule has shortened the long northern winter by 24 joyful days.

Frumity Night and Luckybirds
Northern England's New Year

Tonight it is the New-Year's night, tomorrow it is the day,
We are come about for our right and our ray(1)
As we us'd to do in old King Henry's day,
Sing, fellows sing, Hagman Heigh.

Hogmanay Song from Richmond, Yorkshire

Any Scot who spent Christmas in the old North Riding of Yorkshire in times past might have been forgiven if he thought Hogmanay had arrived a week early. On Christmas morning his hosts waited anxiously for their first visitor, who had to be a dark-haired male, carrying a piece of bread, a lump of coal and a coin. It was Scottish first-footing down to the last detail, except that here they called him the 'Lucky Bird'. Boys and girls joined in as Lucky Birds too, knocking at houses chanting:

I wish you a Merry Christmas and a Happy New Year.
Please may I be the Lucky Bird here?

'The same clamorous singing as on Christmas day commences just as early on New Year's morn, greetings for the new year are as freely given,' wrote Yorkshire folklore authority Richard Blakeborough. House-holders were called to their doors with cries of:

I wish you health and strength and a Happy New Year.

(1) money

Please may I be the Lucky Bird here?

The Lucky Bird tradition neatly bridges the gap between Christmas and New Year and between the English and the Scottish Yule celebration. The similiarity doesn't end there; in England it was called the Festival of Fools, corresponding to the Scottish Daft Days And the merriment, pranks and ploys which people got up to were very similar in both countries.

Preparations for Christmas were identical to the traditional preliminaries for Hogmanay across the Cheviots. On Christmas Eve houses were scrubbed and polished; rowans and evergreens were brought in to decorate them and ward off evil spirits.

From the Dales right across Yorkshire to the coast at Filey people ate a kind of wheatmeal porridge which they called Frumentie or Frumity, and the remains of the Frumity was eaten on New Year's Eve, which consequently was called Frumity Night.

As Richard Blakeborough explains, people observed New Year: 'The older people always watch the old year out and the new year in, which is made known by the ringing of the church bells and the loud knocking at your door of the first-foot or lucky bird. This happens immediately on the last stroke of twelve.' He adds that 'The festive season itself lasts pretty well on towards the middle of the month.' In England folk were clearly just as reluctant to allow their Festival of Fools to come to an end as the Scots were.

Folk were equally enthusiastic about New Year's Eve on both sides of the Pennines, and the nearer to the Border the more Scottish the complexion of the festivities became, with the whisky bottle substituted for gin, ale, or elderberry wine.

Writing in the early part of the present century, the Rector of Ford in Northumberland told how children of the village went guising from door to door, chanting the popular 'Get up guid wife and shake your feathers' rhyme. They called at every dwelling from the big house to shepherds' cottages and were given money, an orange, and (so the good Rector tells us) 'a kind word'. They acted the Goloshan play, but even at that time the young population of the area was dwindling, so that guising and the other rites of New Year were dying out.

Further south guising took the form of mumming. On New Year's Day it was the custom throughout the northern counties for youths to dress up in strange clothes — often women's dress — or, if they could lay hands on no suitable disguise, to put their own clothes on inside out or back to front. With faces blackened, they went round the houses carrying brooms, dusters and dustpans, knocking at every door. As each door was opened they rushed into the house and ran round and round miming cleaning actions and humming continuously through closed lips. Having 'swept away' the old year to make way for the new, they were rewarded with money and moved on to the next house.

In her book, *North Country Traditions*, Joan Poulson recounts a story told by an old woman at Wharton in Cheshire of an unexpected visit by the mummers at the beginning of the century.

> *It occurred one Friday evening and her parents had gone to play whist with friends in the village. It was bath-night and, as she was youngest at eight years of age, she was the last to take her turn. Her elder brothers and sisters were already in bed as she sat in the bath which had been placed in its usual spot before the fire earlier in the evening. "It was New Year time and I was well and truly soaked in the bath*

*when in rushed the mummers. Our doors were never locked
of course. I grabbed the towel around me, but they just carried on and did everything as usual. I couldn't give them any
money as I couldn't get out of the bath".*

The First World War and the social upheaval that followed it put
paid to mumming and to many of the other customs of the Yule period.

The northern Yule was all a mixter-maxter of English and Scottish
custom, superstition and rite, Lucky Birds, waits and wassailing at Christmas and guising and first-footing at New Year. On New Year's morning
the wassail bowl was passed round the villages of the north-east, sometimes carried by girls, at other times by young men. At each house they
stopped to wish the householders a Happy New Year and sang:

> *Wassail, wassail, all over the town,*
> *Our toast it is white, our ale it is brown*
> *Our bowl it is made of a maplin tree,*
> *We be good fellows all, I drink to thee.*

On the western border, in Cumberland, children went from house
to house singing what has been described as 'a sort of carol' and expected to be rewarded with a gift of money or food. Their song began:

> *Hagnuna, Trolola.*
> *Give us some pie,*
> *And let us go away.*

This is the old 'Hogmanay, Trololay' rhyme in yet another part of
the country.

This use of the name Hogmanay appears to be rather less common
in Cumbria than in Northumberland, although first-footing formed —
and still does form — the keystone of the Cumbrian New Year celebration, with the same insistence of having a dark man first scross the threshold. Miss Marjorie Metcalfe, writing from Ulverston, recalled the festivities in the Ravenglass area during the 1960s:

> *Each year after meeting up as just a few folks on New
> Year's Eve, more and more would tag on until there could be*

twenty to thirty folks collected. Hopefully one person would be dark or as known around here 'swarthy'. There was joviality around the streets, and a must was to call at the famous Penington Arms pub in the centre of Ravenglass, where there was more joviality, mince pies, drinks and much singing of folk songs and hunting songs. One song which was always sung was 'The Horn of the Hunter is silent'. This put everyone in the right mood for going from house to house knocking on doors in Ravenglass and the surrounding area, where they were always invited in for a drink and mince pies or something of that sort. They called at every house from the big house, the Hartleys, to the shepherd's cottage at Muncaster Castle. There was still room for fish and chips in between!

On New Year's Eve the keeper of the pound for stray cattle at Richmond, Yorkshire, went round the town pursued by a rabble, knocking on doors and singing what was described by Richard Blakeborough, Richmond's historian, as 'a barbarous song'. This went:

> *Tonight it is the New-Year's night, tomorrow it is the day,*
> *And we are come for our right and for our ray,*
> *As we used to do in old King Henry's day.*
> *Sing, fellows, sing, Hagman Heigh.*
> *If you go to the bacon flick(1), cut me a good bit;*
> *Cut, cut and low beware of your maw;*
> *Cut, cut and round, beware of your thumb,*
> *That me and my merry men may have some.*
> *Sing, fellows, sing. Hagman-heigh.*
> *If you go to the black-ark, bring me an X mark;*
> *Ten mark, ten pound, throw it down upon the ground,*
> *That me and my merry men may have some,*
> *Sing, fellows, sing. Hagman-heigh.*

During the twelve days of Christmas, Richmond's 'daft days', young men of the town, dressed up in shirts ornamented with ribbons folded into roses, and danced a sword dance around the town, collecting money

(1) flitch

from door to door to pay for a feast which they held later in the evening.

They were always accompanied by a fiddler and by two figures who were remnants of the ancient Festival of Fools — a man dressed as a grotesque old woman and called Bessy, and a Fool, who wore furs and a hat with a fox tail dangling from it, Davy Crockett style.

The sword dance was a wildly dangerous kind of morris dance in which the performers carried drawn swords, either real or wooden. As they danced in circles and formed figures they flourished their swords and grasped dangerously at each other's weapons, singing as they danced. In other parts of Yorkshire youths went from village to village dancing a similar sword dance on St Stephen's Day, the day after Christmas.

Not every New Year custom can be traced back to Druids, Vikings or even the Feast of Fools of the Middle Ages; at Tynemouth they fire a gun at the change of the year as part of a ceremony which started only in 1863.

At that time a gun stood on Ballast Hill at North Shields, and was fired at one o'clock each day like Edinburgh's famous One O'Clock Gun. In 1863 it was decided to fire the Ballast Hill gun at midnight on New Year's Eve, and the custom continued until 1903 when the gun was taken away. A local family then arranged for a rocket to be fired each year, a custom which continued until the mid-1950s when the Tynemouth rocket hit the headlines because it crashed through the roof of the town's Welfare Department buildings. That was the end of the Tynemouth rocket, but the borough continues to herald the New Year with a standard maroon flare of the type used to call out the local lifeboat — but they fire it from the safety of the Spanish Battery at Tynemouth, well away from built-up areas.

Noise, fire and light are the three great elements of the Yule festival and at Allendale, on the borders of Northumbria and Cumbria, they hold a fire ceremony which attracts many spectators. Young men of the town, wearing fancy dress, carry barrels on their heads in procession round the town, led by the town band. The barrels are filled with wood shavings and other combustible materials and at the town square a torch made from a charred remnant of the previous year's bonfire is put to each barrel to set it alight. Carrying the blazing barrels on their heads, the men continue to walk in procession round the town, then return to the Square where they toss the blazing barrels onto a huge bonfire.

Twelfth Night brought the northern festive season to its official

end with a celebration during which a cake was cut and handed round. Baked inside were the traditional bean and pea, whose finders became King and Queen for the evening, with powers to order their subjects to dance or perform any comical or outlandish feats they chose. For these final hours of the festival the King and Queen ruled, but soon it came time to end the dancing, to go home, throw out all the green decorations and prepare for work again.

There was one more fling before they called it a day: on Plough Monday, the first Monday after Twelfth Night, when ploughing began, a plough was pulled round the village by young men nicknamed Plough Stots (Plough Oxen). As at Christmas and New Year they festooned themselves in sashes and ribbon roses and were accompanied by other young men in weird costumes. Accompanied by sword dancers and a band or at very least a single fiddler they paraded round the village rattling boxes and demanding money. Those who gave were cheered, but where they received nothing the plough stots shouted, 'Hunger and starvation' and were liable to plough up the path in front of the house! Money collected was spent on a feast or a dance, which really brought the festival to an end. Next day it was (literally) back to the plough for everybody.

Handselling the New Year

They waited till the Auld Kirk bell
Struck twal' then at the final knell,
The laddies a' set up a yell -
'Hurrah for Handsel Monday.'

Handsel Monday, R Anderson

Although people settled on 31 December for their Hogmanay festival, there was much confusion following the adoption of the New Style calendar in 1752. This upset the reckoning for dating Hogmanay, New Year's Day, Uphalieday and all the other landmarks of the Yule holiday. To this day some rites follow the new calendar and some the old one, so that it is possible to celebrate two New Years, the generally accepted one by the modern calendar and the Old or Auld New Year eleven days later.

Stonehaven's brilliant fireball festival lights up the new style Hogmanay, but the north-east's second great fire festival, at Burghead on the Moray coast, takes place on the last day of the year in the old style. Burghead's Burning of the Clavie is the continuation of the ancient fire ceremony to ensure successful fishing in the year ahead. The Clavie is a barrel filled with wood and tar, fixed on the end of a long wooden pole and set alight. Once the Clavie was carried all the way round the town by one man — a tremendous feat of strength — but now a team of men share the task. It is a dangerous job, for burning tar trickles down the back of the man holding it and one stumble can mean disaster both for the carrier and for the town because it is considered a bad omen for the Clavie to be dropped.

The Clavie is no longer taken round the boats in the harbour as in former days, but is borne to the top of Doorie Hill and placed in a special stone cradle. As the fire dies out, there is a mad scramble to grab a charred remnant of the Clavie, which is believed to bring good luck.

The 1752 change in the calendar upset the principal holiday of the working people, which traditionally was held, not on New Year's Day, but on the first Monday after New Year, and called Handsel Monday because that was the day on which workers were given presents by their masters just as they had at Christmas before the Reformation. Handsel Monday could fall on any date between 8 and 19 January, depending on whether one followed the old or the new calendar, which caused confusion for generations.

Until recent times this was a far more important day than either Hogmanay or Ne'erday because it was the only holiday workers were allowed in the entire twelve months, apart from an occasional local fair day. Handsel Monday was like Hogmanay all over again, only better for the poor. It was almost the only time families and friends met, the only day when everybody had a copper to spend and those who wanted to settle to family life had free time to get married. Servants and workers at the bottom of the social ladder looked forward to Handsel Monday for a whole year and they made sure they did not miss a moment of its enjoyment.

In the weaving shops of towns like Dunfermline, men and women worked long additional hours during the weeks prior to the holiday, shuttles racing, in what was called locally the Handsel Monday 'push', to earn extra money for their festivities.

Although it was considered unlucky to get out of bed too early on Handsel Monday because fairies and witches were about on that morning, the fun began soon after midnight, with young people parading through the streets carrying flaming torches, and rousing the town with their singing, blowing tin horns or playing fiddles. No one could lie in bed and ignore the festivities because the whole place reverberated to all this noise.

After this procession they rushed away to breakfast. In the country, farmers laid on a special meal for their workers, while in the towns, factory owners gave a feast for their journeymen, apprentices and servants. The table was laden with ashets of boiled and roasted meat, followed by cheese, oatcakes, currant bun and shortbread, all washed down with Het Pint, ale or whisky.

At the end of the meal handsels or presents, generally of money, were handed out and the workmen and women set out to spend this on luxuries such as they could not even to dream of through the rest of the year.

A distinction must be made between the Hogmanay gift and the Handsel Monday one: the Hogmanay present was a gift pure and simple, but the Handsel one was regarded as part of a servant's wages and was expected as a right. Even schoolmasters were given a handsel by their pupils, and in the Borders the boy and girl who gave most were declared King and Queen of the festivities and could claim that day as a holiday. George Scott, who attended school first at Deanburnhaugh and then at Roberton, near Hawick, in the 1840s, described the practice:

> *Handsel Monday was held at Roberton as well as Deanburnhaugh, and the offerings were very much larger, and after they were counted, we had what we considered a rare treat — a cistern piping hot, a small tray on which was a dozen wine glasses, a larger tray laden with nackets (small cakes) and each scholar received a glass of toddy and a nacket and were then dismissed on holiday.*

When they had spent their money, the vast majority of workers enjoyed the rest of the day with their families or playing all those games which are associated with New Year's Day — running races, football, feats of strength, ice hockey on the lochs if the weather were severe enough, and even cock-fighting.

Cock-fighting was very common up to the mid-1800s in areas as far apart as the Borders, Fife and Perthshire and the school playground was even used as the cock-pit. Recalling Dunfermline district in the 1830s, Joseph Hutton wrote: 'The very village schools were turned into cock-pits at the Handsel Monday time, the schoolmaster getting some o' the killed cocks for the use o' the school.'

By the time Hutton wrote this, things had improved: 'Instead of the fighting of cocks, you have on New Year's Day the Ornithological Society. An exhibition takes place in the Music Hall every New Year Day, when hundreds feast their eyes with delight and spend a very agreeable hour or two gazing with admiration on the feathered race. That is surely a decided change to the better.'

Gazing on the 'feathered race' or watching members of it tearing each other apart; there were many who sought alternative entertainments. The minister of Currie, Midlothian, told how his parishioners spent Handsel Monday in 1845:

> *The annual fair and Old Handsel Monday are the only periodical holidays for the working classes, on which latter occasion the servants enjoy the pleasure of returning to the bosom of their families, and spending the close of the day with their friends. The early part is generally devoted to the less innocent amusement of raffles and shooting with firearms, which, being often old and rusty, as well as wielded by inexperienced hands, have occasioned some disagreeable accidents.*

As celebrations became wilder towards the middle of the nineteenth century, abstinence societies tried, often vainly, to bring some order to Handsel Monday. Good thoughts and good deeds were reflected in mid-century reports of the celebrations. The *Dunfermline Journal* (January 1851) reported many events in the town for Handsel Monday which fell that year on 13 January. The 143 inmates of the Poor House were given a dinner, at which they were served beef; the newspaper commented, 'We are certain no better butcher meat was placed on the table of any gentleman in the town.' Toasts (drunk in an unspecified beverage) tempered the joy; they contained feeling references to those who had attended former dinners 'but who had been removed by the cold hand of death', and awful warnings to be prepared for whatever might happen! Apprentices got off more lightly; they were reminded of the necessity of 'truthfulness, honesty, sobriety and frugality'.

Shops were shut either for the whole day or at least for the afternoon and in the evening the Total Abstinence Society held a soiree in a packed Masons' Hall, during which five temperance lectures were interspersed with 'temperance melodies sung in good style by the Juvenile Tee-Total Band'. The town's Juvenile Abstainers held their own entertainment attended by 400, and 600 people crowded into the Masons' Hall the following evening for yet another teetotal entertainment.

On a less morally elevated (but possibly more popular) level, concerts and dances were held throughout the week. Many workers extended their holiday to Handsel Tuesday, which was the day on which ploughmen and servant girls came into the town to spend their handsel gift money and stayed on to enjoy the dances and other entertainments in public halls or in private houses. Nearly everywhere people kept open house so that strangers were welcome to join in the family festivities.

One way or another, many folk managed to extend the Handsel Monday fun to as much as a whole week off. Pressure grew to regularise the holiday and combine the Handsel Monday festivities with New Year, but many resisted, particularly the poor who feared they might lose their holiday and their presents altogether. Both Kirkcaldy and Dunfermline fought a rearguard action against change for longer than most other places, but the tide could not be stopped and gradually all Scotland came to observe New Year's Day as the festival. Dunfermline capitulated only in 1870, but even then a group of young men formed an Auld Handsel Monday Association which met each year to hold its own Handsel Monday celebration. Dunfermline exiles in other parts of Scotland and as far away as London also held similar meetings.

Handsel Monday lingered in agricultural areas until the turn of the century when the *Haddington Courier* listed the Handsel Monday events, whilst at the same time bemoaning the decline of the holiday. In 1894 it recorded no fewer than twenty Handsel Monday events — shooting matches at Gifford and Garvald, games at East Linton, an ornithological show at Aberlady, balls at Ballencrieff, East Linton, Gifford, Aberlady and Stenton, where festoons of evergreens picked out with camellias were hung gracefully round the walls and pink and white chains were suspended from the ceiling. And although it was work as usual on the following day, more than fifty couples danced the night away until five in the morning at Gifford.

Farm and estate workers were given traditional handsels. At Abbeymains each received 'a sum of money and a cut of mutton'. Castlemains' servants were given 'a currant loaf and a quantity of tea' through the kindness of Lord Tweeddale, and the farmer at Archerfield presented each of his workers with a leg of mutton. Handsel Monday presents were not confined to the farming fraternity; at East Linton that year fifty tons of coal were distributed among the deserving poor, while the parish minister 'with characteristic kindly thought went round the

village at the end of the week and distributed tea and other articles to many of the poor'.

From village to village and town to town enthusiasm varied. At Aberlady, the *Courier* reported, the day was held 'in the good old-fashioned style...and it seems as if it will die hard here if it has to die at all'. Dunbar was half-hearted and in North Berwick the holiday was no more than a memory. A barn dance at North Berwick Mains was not enough to save the town's reputation. The paper wrote, 'Auld Handsel Monday is nothing more than a name in North Berwick. Time was when racing and other games were extremely popular on the links here, but of late years the observance of the day has rapidly declined, and on Monday it may be said to have been unobserved here but for the presence at the cross of swing-boats and other itinerant attractions'.

Pencaitland was becoming 'quieter year by year', Saltoun had none of the customary Handsel Monday spirit, while at Cockenzie the celebration was a thing of the past. Once again a Hogmanay tradition had moved on, deplored but soon accepted, just as change had always been complained about but acceded to every since the mid-winter festival began.

Resolutions — to Keep and to Break

*The practice of making resolutions
on New Year's Eve was a Victorian
invention, introduced by maudlin
Scots and sentimental dissenters.*

Philip Howard, The Times, 1983

Hogmanay is a time to look forward and — for us Scots who are a sentimental race — to look back. It is a moment to restore one's spirits and renew hopes for the future. Resolutions are a part of that.

And yet, and yet...while I have been compiling this *Hogmanay Companion* not a single person to whom I have spoken or with whom I have corresponded has mentioned *New Year Resolutions*. Books of memories, rites and customs are silent about them, too, as are those principal authorities on superstitions, rites and festivals, Sir James Frazer's *Golden Bough* and F Marian McNeill's *Silver Bough*.

Yet resolutions are on everyone's lips on New Year's Day; one of the most common questions asked at this time is, 'Have you made your New Year's resolutions?' On the day after this becomes, 'Have you broken them yet?' Many people make resolutions one day and break them the next, it is true, yet that is surely better than the efforts our ancestors made to improve their lives at Yule.

The Celts left no sign that they determined at that time of the year to erect higher standing stones; not a whisper has come down from the Romans to suggest that during their Saturnalia they resolved to throw

fewer captives to the lions and no evidence exists to show that Vikings promised to refrain henceforth from pillaging monasteries. Christians of the Middle Ages were no better, and certainly the Presbyterians and Puritans of later centuries saw little need for resolutions — the *good* life was to be lived 365 days of the year.

Can it be that resolutions are just an invention of our impious backsliding age, a Victorian invention as the writer Philip Howard suggests? Did our great-great-grandparents add a resolve to do better in the year ahead to their Hogmanay rites as they saw other, older customs fade? Robert Chambers in his *Book of Days,* published in 1862, gives the game away when he quotes from the *Mirror of the Months*:

> *Every first of January that we arrive at, is an imaginary milestone on the turnpike track of human life: at once a resting-place for thought and meditations, and a starting point for fresh exertion in the performance of our journey. The man who does not at least* propose to himself *to be better* this *year than he was last, must be either very good or very bad indeed! And only to* propose *to be better, is something; if noth-*

ing else, it is an acknowledgment of our need to be so, which is the first step towards amendment.

How splendidly Victorian! The old Queen herself couldn't have put it better. If the New Year Resolution was a Victorian invention, it was a brilliant one, because it lies in perfect harmony with that seam of sentimentality that runs through the sternest Scottish character.

Through recent generations we have become a race of 'resolvers', determined to improve ourselves, and there can be no better moment on which to make such a resolve than the start of the New Year. It was already part of the Yuletide tradition to clean our homes, pay our bills, and start anew, so why not determine to improve ourselves as well in the process?

It might be argued, as Chambers does, that a resolution — even a broken resolution — must show good intent at the very least. No doubt it does, but having made our resolutions, surely it is better to raise a glass and drink to them, then get on with living in the year ahead.

> *And let us wish that ane an' a'*
> *Our friends baith far and near*
> *May aye enjoy in times to come*
> *A hearty guid New year.*

New Years Ahead

Weel may we a' be,
Ill may we never see,
Here's to the King
And guid companie!

Jacobite toast

No wonder the Scottish New Year is unique: a magical time, when we gather together, shake hands with the enthusiasm of the French, drink as deeply and solemnly as Russians and disappear for days into a haze of alcohol and wellbeing. The chime of midnight is a moment which can never be created at any other time because it touches the spirit of the Scots in a way that nothing else can.

For generations, unseen, unfathomable forces drove us to scrub our homes and tidy up our lives on the last day of the year in preparation for a new start. Every corner of the house was swept, every surface polished until it glowed, all dishes were washed and the doorstep was given such a thorough scrubbing that the whole family could eat their New Year's Day dinner off it.

People buffed their lives to a glossy sheen as well, setting aside old enmities (if not actually forgetting them!), paying their bills (or as many as they could) and resolving to lead a different (and more purposeful) life. And so it has been since time immemorial, for Hogmanay is a festival as old as the hills.

As old as the hills, but not what it used to be. Every Scot has heard his or her grannie say, 'It wasna' like that in my day.' And she was right — Hogmanay never was the same as it was a generation before. Hogmanay has been in a process of change since history began — from the ancient mid-winter solstice feast to Roman Saturnalia, Norsemen's Yule, mediaeval Christmas and Hogmanay, a celebration barely tolerated after the puritanical authorities banned Christmas. Generations absorbed this evolution, ever complaining, but always adapting to it. The present day is no different. There are endless complaints about excessive drinking and older people look back to their youth as a gentler, more reasonable, more sober age.

More sober age? It comes as a shock then to read of wild Hogmanays in the past. In *The Book of Days*, Robert Chambers recounts how a group of youths waylaid first-footers in Edinburgh in 1812 and a policeman and a young clerk were fatally injured. Three of the youths were tried and executed and, according to Chambers, the old custom of first-footing began to fall off after that. People are still saying today that first-footing is declining because streets are less safe.

In the present century, two world wars, the depression years of the 1930s and the more affluent second half of the century have all had their effect. Hogmanay in towns and cities during these times may have been wild and noisy, but on the whole they have remained remarkably good-tempered and with relatively little crime.

The 1970s and 1980s altered the Scottish Hogmanay again. These decades brought changes which have shaken the festival as fundamentally as the Reformation did four centuries ago. This time the catalyst has not been the Church or any other authority. No law has been passed to forbid its celebration. Hogmanay has moved on simply in response to evolving living patterns.

Christmas, Hogmanay and New Year have merged into a single celebration, taking us back to the ancient Yuletide or the Twelve Days of Christmas. In Scotland a century or more ago a New Year holiday (not necessarily observed on 1 January) was the only break domestic servants and other workers were allowed in winter. After the Second World War, New Year's Day became a general holiday, with many factories and offices taking 2 January off as well.

Christmas began to be more widely observed in Scotland from the 1950s on, but it was only in the 1960s that it became an officially recognised holiday north of the Border. In England New Year's Day is now a public holiday, too, but only because it was imposed there by the European Community.

Resulting from this, the days between Christmas and New Year became 'dead days' when it was hard to concentrate on work, so a number of factories chose to stop production and give their workforce the whole week off. Office workers also started to have more annual holidays, spread across the year, so that they could save a few days to tack on to Christmas and create a break of ten days or even a fortnight.

With higher incomes at their disposal than their parents ever dreamt of, many now are able to take advantage of fast, cheap and easy travel to fly off to Majorca or Miami for a holiday at this time. Others visit family as far away as America or Australia at the Christmas/New Year season. They take the Scottish Hogmanay customs with them so that as Scotland loses, the world gains.

The daily lifestyle of Scots has altered greatly in recent years, too, and this has had its effect on the manner in which we celebrate New Year. As many people from the south or from other countries settle in Scotland, we find that, even in small communites, neighbours are often hardly known to one another. Incomers do not know the traditions of the orthodox Scottish Hogmanay, so consequently the festival is no longer the community affair it once was.

Only a generation ago, complete strangers were welcome as first-footers at virtually any house, but now, because of growing crime rates, an uninvited stranger is unlikely to be welcomed in as he would have once been. This is the price of progress, and those of us who are old enough to remember past Hogmanays regret it.

In country districts there has been social change, too. In remoter areas many of the younger folk have left to live in towns, but that is not a new problem. What is new is the change which has taken place in farming, resulting in cottages and even farmhouses being sold off. Newcomers from the towns who now live in these have no idea how to celebrate Hogmanay, however anxious they may be to fit into the community. They know about first-footing, but even if they would like to go round their neighbours on Hogmanay, that would be difficult, since people are no longer prepared to walk distances and they cannot drink and drive. Consequently, they stay at home.

One feature of life common to town and country, which has had a staggering impact on the way in which Hogmanay is celebrated, is television. As the little box in the corner of the living room has come to dominate life throughout the year in the majority of homes, it has also taken over New Year. For many years the BBC and commercial television channels made a great feature of the Scottishness of Hogmanay and put on a special show which attracted millions of viewers. The television set came to be the clock which timed the arrival of the New Year, taking the place of the town clock or kirk bells of the old days. And the first hour of the New Year, which was devoted to bagpipes, Scottish dancing and songs from the best-known Scottish entertainers, stamped *Scotland* on the celebration.

New Year is no longer a purely Scottish holiday; it is observed officially as a day off in almost every major country around the world, including England, so Scotland has to share her unique festival. The television companies have taken their cue from this and the programmes they offer even to viewers in Scotland on Hogmanay are a wan shadow of what they were in the 1970s and early 1980s. Hogmanay has become New Year's Eve, and the result has been to dilute the Scottishness of Scotland's own festival.

Native Scots have not helped. Many have forgotten the superstitions and rites associated with Hogmanay. Houses are rarely scrubbed and polished in preparation, nowadays debts are carried over from one year to another, and it is no longer considered a disgrace to start the New Year owing anything to anyone. There is no longer a housewife to be found in the whole of Glasgow who rushes to the close mouth with the ashes from her fire at two minutes to twelve!

It is little wonder then that Hogmanay has become a festival to be celebrated in the pub, club, or privately, within the home. But even in these places, our grannies would say Hogmanay is not what it used to be. A generation ago New Year was the only time in the whole twelve months from January to December at which many people drank in any quantity; today a great number celebrate 52 (or more) Hogmanays every year. People, especially among the younger generation, drink more throughout the year, and many have not learned to control their drinking. They perceive Hogmanay as a great orgy of overindulgence and on the morning of New Year's Day a great silence descends because much of the country is too hung over to face the traditional New Year's Day.

This has given Hogmanay's critics an excuse to encourage people to celebrate Christmas instead of New Year, yet anyone who has lived in England can testify to the fact that the same alcohol problem exists there at Christmastime. The problem is an immense one with little relation to

Hogmanay, but one thing is sure, its solution does not lie in abandoning a celebration which has been a part of Scottish life since time immemorial.

But do not despair, there is plenty of evidence that many of the traditions of the Scottish Hogmanay still survive. It is still the one time when families spend time together. Hogmanay is a very special name for a very special festival, and in spite of the way in which modern life has diluted it, it remains uniquely Scottish.

Hogmanay will not die because it is a part of the Scots ethos — and that spirit is stronger then ever today, despite all the forces ranged against it. It has survived for four centuries of shared monarchy with England and three of shared parliament. Fortunately the Treaty of Union, which united Scotland and England in 1707, left Scotland with its own Church and legal and educational systems, and it instilled a radical nationalistic spirit in the country which continues to flourish. The secret of Hogmanay's survival lies in the fact that history has not managed to smother that hopeless romantic strain inherent in the Scottish character. We are happy to share England's Christmas, but we are damned if we will lose our own New Year in the process!

Scotland's enduring Scottishness offers us the best hope of ensuring that New Year will continue to be celebrated. Hogmanay, with all its changes, will continue to be a vital festival in the social calendar with time-honoured customs, which we may not be able to explain, but will continue to observe.

At the end of the twentieth century, Scotland still wishes the world a happy Hogmanay, a guid New Year and mony o' them.

Part Two

A Guid New Year Party

The damsel donned her kirtle sheen,
The hall was dressed with holly green,
Forth to the wood did merry-men go
To gather in the mistletoe.

Marmion, Sir Walter Scott, 1808

Your Hogmanay party is much more than a gathering of friends and family; it is invitation to participate in perpetuating an ancient, unbroken tradition. Hogmanay is fun, but it also has a serious aspect because it is a moment to pause to assess one's life and to move forward in new directions.

Non-Scots incline to dismiss Burns Night as an excuse to eat outlandish food, swill whisky and listen to endless self-praise; those same people call Hogmanay a godless Christmas celebrated to excess. How wrong they are!

To Scots it is important to celebrate Hogmanay and, in doing so, to continue customs which have been handed down through countless generations. It doesn't matter that these have changed. What does count is that the idea behind the custom should be carried on into the next generation.

Your Hogmanay party therefore must include or reflect as many of the elements of that tradition as possible. Make the customs a part of the event, explain them to your guests, and you will be astonished by the new dimension it will give the celebration. People always respond to their own heritage even if they have all but forgotten it, and outsiders are fascinated by it, so all will appreciate and remember the year they helped you to welcome in the New Year in Scottish style. Better still, they may adopt the customs you have taught them and help to spread the Hogmanay traditions to other parts.

GREENERY AND LIGHT

Decorating the house the house in past times was a key preparation for Yule celebrations. Mistletoe, holly, rowan, juniper and other evergreens should all be used — particularly rowan over the door lintels and plenty of holly for good luck, as well as mistletoe, the traditional fertility symbol. But don't forget, you will break the good luck if you leave them up after Twelfth Night, so remember to take them down before 6 January — which will give you an excuse for another party!

Gather as many of these elements together to decorate your house for Hogmanay, but be sure to explain to your guests that this is not just a whim on your part: each custom has its reason. Pin up a list for guests to read the meanings of the various plants. It might read something like this:

EVERGREEN MAGIC

Our ancestors hung evergreens in their houses at Yuletide as a promise that spring would soon return:

rowan for luck;

holly for luck and good health as well;

sacred Mistletoe for fertility and to ward off witches or evil spirits;

juniper to cleanse.

Light formed an important element of the ancient Yule celebration, as it still does in many places. Use candles and other lights to demonstrate that you, too, recognise the power of the sun just as your ancestors did and that you are grateful that it has now passed the solstice and is returning to bring its life-giving powers to the world.

You can't fill the house with blazing torches as our Viking forebears did, but you can at least set plenty of candles or decorative lights in the windows and around each room.

THE PARTY THEME

Dressing up and guising are associated much more with Hallowe'en than with Hogmanay nowadays, yet in the past they were part of the Daft Days. People at every level of Scottish social life, from the King and Queen to the poorest country folk, dressed up in fancy costumes and took part in games and guising. The rich dressed up merely for fun; the poor did it to collect food for their Hogmanay feast.

Guising has all but vanished as part of Scotland's Hogmanay revelries, which is an excellent reason for you to bring it back. Make your Hogmanay party fancy dress, explaining on the invitation that this is not just a notion on your part, but the perpetuation of an ancient custom.

Strangers would be surprised to have guisers calling at their doors chanting the ancient 'Get up, good wife, and shake your feathers' rhyme on Hogmanay, but neighbours who have been forewarned might enjoy the novelty. Perhaps you could persuade the children and a few of your adult guests to go round selected houses of neighbours as a token revival of guising. They may even bring back a little in the way of food or drink to 'fuel' the party spirit. They will certainly return better attuned to what Hogmanay is all about.

TWELFTH NIGHT, HANDSEL MONDAY OR UPHALIEDAY PARTY

To round off the Yule festivities you could hold a party for Twelfth Night (Uphalieday) or Handsel Monday.

Twelfth Night

The Scots called this Uphalieday. It was the traditional end of the Christmas festivities, and it was a night for fancy dress and dancing. A man and a woman were chosen as King and Queen of the Bean and they had supreme power for the evening. Make your Twelfth Night party a fancy dress one, and appoint a King and Queen of the Bean to be masters of ceremonies.

Make a small bun or tart for each guest. Hide a dried bean in one and a pea in another (wrapped in paper so that they won't be swallowed accidentally) and the man and woman who get the bun with the bean and the pea will be King and Queen of the Bean.

Last thing before the guests leave, you must take down all the decorations and greenery to show that Yule is over. This is always a moment tinged with regret that the 'party' is over.

Handsel Monday

Since the first Monday after New Year was a holiday for working men and women when they were given presents by their masters, a suitable Handsel Monday Party theme would be to provide a small present for each guest, or ask each guest to bring a small mystery parcel. These could be exchanged as part of a game, or set in a pile in the middle of the room and handed out as rewards for performing a forfeit.

PLANNING THE PARTY

A good Hogmanay party begins with a plan which has been laid at least a month to six weeks in advance. If you don't draw up a plan, you will spend anxious days between Christmas and New Year wondering how many guests to cater for and on Hogmanay itself you may well run out of the party spirit — quite literally!

Draw up a plan, follow it, delegate as much of the organising work as you can to members of the family, and don't worry. Your Hogmanay party is for you to enjoy just as much as your guests.

Draw up a check list and tick off each item as it is attended to. An example is given overleaf.

WHO'S COMING

How many people make up a quorum for a Hogmanay party — two can manage very well — so can a few hundred! It all depends on the type of party you like, the amount of space available, and — of course, how many friends you have. For a sit-down dinner party you may want only eight or ten guests at the most, but twice as many could be accommodated for a buffet supper or a drinks party.

You know how many people your house will hold and how many more can be squeezed in if you remove larger pieces of furniture from the room, or make your guests stand rather than sit. However Hogmanay is a marathon celebration which goes on for a long time, so do

CHECK LIST

	Action	Completed
Date/Time		
Guest List		
Invitations ordered/written		
Invitations posted		
Decorations		
Candles		

Food required

1 ....
2 ....
3 ....
4 ....
5 ....

Drinks required

1 ....
2 ....
3 ....
4 ....
5 ....

Ice
Glasses/paper cups
Music
China/paper plates
Cutlery
Napkins
Prizes/gifts
Corkscrews

provide some seating arrangements. Don't invite the whole neighbour-hood: the party grapevine has long roots and word gets around, so it is better to hold a few invitations back to send out in the event of refusals.

WHEN?

Timing is crucial on Hogmanay night. Remember, the celebration goes on into the 'wee sma' 'oors', so don't invite your guests too early.

If you are serving dinner 8.30 for 9.00pm is time enough. For a buffet party or a drinks party 9.30 or even 10pm is quite early enough. Remember that the English always arrive on time' the Scots and Irish come late.

THE INVITATION

The first essential is to make sure that your party doesn't clash with someone else's. Check with key guests in plenty of time, certainly no later than early November. Send out your invitations good and early because the most entertaining guests will receive lots of invitations. Four

weeks ahead is the generally accepted time. You could post them all at the same time as you post your Christmas cards — or even put them in with your cards to save postage.

The invitation can be anything from a handwritten letter to those printed cards you can buy in packs of six or ten at a stationer's shop. You can personalise your invitations and make them reflect the party theme. A home-made typed card with a tartan ribbon attached to it would be appropriate or, if cost is no object and the party is more formal, you could have a card specially designed.

In these days of photocopying and quick print shops you can devise your own special invitation and have it printed inexpensively. Draw a design or get an artistic friend to make one and hand letter the wording, then have the requisite number of copies run off.

The invitation must give the date, time and place of the party as well as say whether it's a dinner, buffet supper, drinks or a 'please bring a bottle' party. It should indicate whether dress is fancy, formal, or informal, and it should ask for a reply — RSVP. Nowadays, when people seem to find it so hard to put pen to paper it is a good idea to include a telephone number for replies. Specimen inviatations can be found on page 100.

MAKING THE PARTY GO

Food and drink suggestions follow in subsequent chapters, so it is unnecessary to say more about them here than that guests should be welcomed with a traditional drink. The Het Pint (recipe: page) is both warming and unusual enough to be a talking point.

The party should then build up to midnight when the New Year is welcomed in with due ceremony — and whisky, of course!

Delegate someone in advance to lead the proceedings through the midnight ceremonial. Just before twelve o'clock strikes he or she should ensure that everybody has a well-filled glass from which to toast the New Year and that an empty glass awaits the family's first-foot.

You can take a chance on who will be your first-foot, but it is safer to arrange in advance for the right person to be first across your threshold. Choose a dark man from among the guests, making sure he has the traditional first-footer's gifts — a piece of coal, something to eat, something to drink, and for good measure a silver coin to ensure prosperity.

A minute or so before midnight the head of the house should open the front door and let the first-footer out to wait until the chime of the clock signals the New Year. As the first-footer enters, all the guests should make as much noise as possible to frighten away bad spirits. provide bells, pots, pans, tin trays and ask everybody to ring or bang these loudly to make a great noise as the first-footer enters. The first-footer will pour a dram from his bottle into the empty glass and offer it to his host with a toast: 'A Guid New Year to ane and a''.

The host should then offer the first-footer a dram and the whole gathering can now start to wish each other a Happy New Year. This is the one night of the year when kissing the opposite sex is allowed. Now the whole assembly forms a circle to sing *A Gude New Year* and *Auld Lang Syne*. (See pages 119-126)

In the old days many guests often left the party as soon as the New Year had been welcomed in to go first-footing at other friends' and neighbours' houses. However, as the celebration of Hogmanay has become less of a communal affair, first-footing is less popular today.

From then on the party continues until every guest feels that the New Year has been fittingly welcomed in. A real Scottish New Year party will be interrupted by a constant ringing of the doorbell as friends and neighbours arrive to wish you a Happy New Year and share a toast to the year ahead. In between there will be Scottish music, songs and dances.

If all the guests leave at the same time, it is appropriate to end with everyone gathered in a circle to hold hands and sing *Auld Lang Syne*. In practice Hogmanay parties seldom finish so tidily; people drift away, others arrive and leave until there comes a moment of stillness when the host is left alone with the last guests. By mutual consent, and usually without a word being uttered, all agree that the New Year has been handsomely ushered in. The music stops; conversation falters, everybody admits exhaustion. The host suggests a nightcap, which is drunk in silence or near silence. Often this is a moment form reminiscence among old friends. It is time for a final 'Happy New Year' and bed.

Good Hogmanay parties never end; they just fade into the dawn of the New Year.

SPECIMEN INVITATIONS

Come guising with us
on Hogmanay
at Our House, 20 Coronation Avenue
at 9 pm
and join us for a Buffet Supper
and help us to welcome in the New Year.

RSVP
Tel: 860.91

John and Betty Brown
20 Coronation Avenue

Guising is an ancient Scottish New Year Custom.
Choose any fancy dress you wish. There will be a
prize for the most original.

A more formal invitation might say:

John and Betty Brown
invite you to a Hogmanay Party
at 20 Coronation Avenue
on Tuesday, 31 December at 9.30 pm

RSVP
20 Coronation Road
Telephone: 860.91

Buffet Supper
Dress Informal

Flour of Scotland
Food for the Party

The flour of Scotland and the fruit of Spain,
Met together in a shower of rain.

Old rhyme on the Hogmanay Clootie Dumpling

What you ate at Ne'erday depended very much on who you were and where you stood on the social scale. For the rich it was a feast fit for a king. For the poor it could be meagre enough, although most communities saw to it that this was the one day on which bellies were well filled.

The New Year dinner developed from the Viking Yule board and the Christmas feast of the Middle Ages. Today's traditional dishes have evolved from delicacies which were served at those earlier feasts. To this day goose is a popular main course for the New Year meal and Black Bun and shortbread have their origins in the ancient Scottish Yule.

The poor rarely saw meat on their table, so their principal food was the Yule bread or oatcakes, usually served with a tasty piece cut from the Yule kebbuck of cheese. This was washed down with a dram or a tankard of specially brewed Yule ale. Whoever came to the house was given a piece of Yule bread and a dram, and to this day a tray of various cakes sits on Scottish sideboards for several days after New Year's Day, waiting to be offered, along with a dram, to every person arriving at the house for the first time that New Year.

Like most housewives, my mother had a special silver cake tray with a handle, which was polished on Hogmanay until it dazzled the eye. This stood on the sideboard in the 'good room' filled with cake carefully wrapped in a napkin to keep it fresh, awaiting the first visitors of the New Year. There was always shortbread (often two kinds), Black Bun, Christmas plum cake, a plainer sultana cake and a cherry cake. Cherry cake was bland enough to offer to folk who had been overindulging for days. It was especially popular with women visitors, most of whom were no mean judges of a cherry cake, for they had been baking them all their lives.

In the past there was no cherry cake and no rich plum cake in humble homes — plain barley bread and oatcakes were the best that could be offered. At New Year these breads were spiked up with fruit and spices and the oatcakes were baked with special care. The large rounds were cut into three large farls or into quarters. A little bacon fat gave a delicious flavour to the oatcakes and the best bakers rolled them so thin they curled up and had to be buttered with tremendous care to avoid breaking them. To accompany the oatcakes an especially good cheese was made and flavoured with caraway seeds.

In some country parts, especially in the north, they made sowans — the gruel which was produced by fermenting the sids or inner husks of the oats which I mentioned in a previous chapter. Sowans was sometimes made special at Hogmanay by the addition of honey, black treacle or even whisky. Today's Atholl Brose could be described as a kind of lineal descendant from the Yule sowans — but considerably up the social scale!

At the royal court and in noble houses the Yuletide feast was very different, often with a boar's head as its centrepiece. Goose, which was the other favourite for the Scottish banquet, was sometimes roasted and sometimes baked in a pie. Pies were a great favourite and the poet Allan Ramsey told how he went to his favourite hostelry at Yuletide to enjoy 'a bra' goose-pie'. Pies and poultry are still inextricably a part of the Scottish New Year. Chicken or even turkey have taken the place of goose in most homes and the traditional Scottish steak pie takes precedence over fowl in many.

After the main dish there followed traditional plum potage or plum porridge, containing meal and various meats and fruits. In time, this became more solid and sweeter and evolved into our plum pudding, which in a Scottish home is known as Clootie Dumpling (a dumpling which is boiled wrapped in a cloth).

For a Hogmanay or New Year's Day feast today this would be a suitable menu:

Venison, Kipper or Salmon Paté
or
Scotch Broth

* * *

Haggis

* * *

Turkey
or
Goose
or
Steak Pie

Cabbage, Turnip & Potatoes

* * *

Clootie Dumpling
or
Trifle
or
Atholl Brose Cream

* * *

Oatcakes and Cheese

INFORMAL DINNER OR BUFFET

On Hogmanay, a good and relatively easy way to ensure a traditional Scottish flavour to the evening is to serve a simple dinner or buf-

fet supper of Haggis with mashed neeps (turnip) and mashed potatoes. Fresh Haggis is relatively easy to come by in almost any part of Britain these days, and it is even sent round the world in tins to satisfy the Scots' longing for their traditional native fare. Canned haggis is not at all bad and for anyone who is far from home at Ne'erday or on Burns Night it is perfectly acceptable. One great advantage of Haggis and a' the trimmings for a Hogmanay party is that it can be prepared in advance and keeps well in the oven until it is served. It is easy to serve from a buffet table as a fork supper.

For dessert, Atholl Brose Cream is a perfect choice, with oatcakes and cheese as a less rich alternative.

DRINKS PARTY

At a Hogmanay drinks party there is no need to serve any food other than crisps and a few canapes — Scotch smoked salmon, kipper and venison patés are appropriate for these, but lesser ingredients will do perfectly well.

However, the centrepiece of the evening should be the traditional Scottish Black Bun. This is really a very moist, very rich cake baked in a pastry crust. Black Bun bought from the shops tends to be more solid and like a cake, but the real test of texture is that it should be so moist it sticks to the knife as it is cut.

Recipes for Hogmanay dishes described above can be found in Appendix I (page 132).

Plenty of Bottle

Drinks for the Party

That merry night we get the corn in
O sweetly, then, thou reams(1) the horn in!
Or reekin(2) on a New-Year mornin
In cog or bicker (3)
An just a wee drap sp'ritual burn in
An gusty sucker (4)

Scotch Drink by Robert Burns

In Scotland they call it 'The Bottle'. 'Hae ye got the Bottle in yet?' people ask earnestly as Hogmanay approaches. 'Ye'll hae a wee dram oot o' the Bottle,' they urge after the preliminaries of welcoming first-footing visitors are over. There is only one bottle — the whisky bottle, the Water of Life or Uisge Beatha to give it its Gaelic name.

Whisky was originally a Highland and Hebridean drink, but today it is Scotland's national tipple from the Cheviots to the Shetlands and a taste which is shared around the world to the point where others are trying to copy it, some quite successfully.

Whisky has been produced in Scotland for centuries, but until the nineteenth Century it was a pretty rough distillation made locally as it was needed for home consumption. It was produced without much care or any of the careful ageing which helps us to enjoy today's whiskies, whether pure malts or blends. In those days folk made their own and

(1) froths; (2) steaming; (3) drinking vessel; (4) tasty sugar

often took a jug of it with them when visiting friends or when going to a ceilidh. This was poured into a communal dish to be shared by all those present. The result must often have been a very peculiar blend!

Whisky today is a very different drink, carefully distilled, smoother, purer, more palatable, and even more warming to the heart than it was a couple of centuries ago. It comes in a wide range of tastes governed by many factors, including raw materials, production methods and blend. The water used is of vital importance; some whiskies have a heavy, peat-rich savour, while others reflect the rocky mountain streams from which the water is drawn to make them.

Whisky is not one drink — it is many subtle tastes, but whatever the character of the final blend, it is a unique drink, inseparable from any Scottish festivity from Burns Night to Hogmanay. It is an essential part of any Scottish party, so even if you are offering other drinks during the evening it is a good idea to mark the Scottishness of the occasion at the start by offering a dram or a whisky punch as a welcoming drink on arrival. Apart from anything else, it will be appreciated by those who are stepping into your house out of a cold winter night. They will appreciate a punch to warm the cockles of their heart!

The Het Pint was the traditional first-footers' drink, carried around in a copper kettle to offer to anybody and everybody one met. It would make a good drink with which to start the party, or to serve later from a pot which could be kept simmering on the stove through the wee sma 'oors to welcome arrivals after midnight (recipe: page 145).

Atholl Brose is another unmistakably Scottish brew for Hogmanay, either as a drink or with whipped cream as a dessert. It has the great advantage that it can be made in advance, but the great disadvantage of being so delicious that it tends to be tried and tasted until only a fraction of the original quantity is left. It is outrageously rich and some people find it too sweet for today's taste, so serve it in very small quantities (recipe: page 147)

A dram is essential to drink the toast to the New Year of course — preferably plain whisky with a dash of water. No drink is more appropriate for the ceremonial bidding of farewell to the old year and the welcoming of the new.

Other than a dram for this key moment, your party drinks can be as varied or restricted as you wish or as your budget allows. If cash is limited, a choice of wines during the evening is perfectly acceptable, or

you might make the event a bottle party to which each guest is asked to contribute a bottle. If you do this, however, talk to your friends in advance and suggest a specific type of spirit or wine which they can bring, otherwise you risk ending up with many bottles of plonk which nobody will enjoy.

Remember that some people may want non-alcoholic drinks. Today people are acutely aware of the importance of not mixing drinking and driving, so do not press alcohol on your guests — not even one at the start of the party. If they say, 'No thanks', accept their decision.

There are plenty of interesting non-alcoholic drinks on the off-licence or supermarket shelves to enable you to have a good selection available. Lemonade, coke, bitter lemon and dry ginger are essential. Orange, pineapple or other fruit (including tropical fruit) juices and mineral water are also good party standbys. There are also innumerable low alcohol beers and wines which are becoming very popular.

And of course ginger wine or cordial is an essential. Time after time while I was working on this Hogmanay Companion people reminisced with affection about the bottle of ginger wine which always sat on the sideboard and which they enjoyed as children. However, ginger wine or cordial is not just a children's drink: it is for guests of any age at any time of the year (recipe: page 147).

Make your party drinks check-list in advance and mark the quantities of each which you will need, remembering any special preferences you know individual guests have. In calculating quantities, remember that you should get about thirty-two glasses of spirits out of a 70 cl bottle and six glasses of wine out of a 75 cl bottle. Here are some suggestions:

SPIRITS
Scotch Whisky
Gin
Vodka
Rum, white & dark
Brandy

WINES
Red and White
(3 litre boxes are convenient)

BEERS
Including non & low-alcohol

SHERRY
Dry
Medium
Sweet

OTHER ALCOHOLIC DRINKS
Campari
Cinzano
Martini
Advocaat, etc

MIXERS
Tonic
Bitter Lemon
Dry Ginger

SOFT DRINKS
Lemonade
Coke
Orange squash/juice
Mineral water

When ordering drinks you can also ask for glasses since most good off-licences will happily lend these free, provided you buy your drinks from them. But if your party is on Hogmanay or any other popular party night, be sure to order early.

Have plenty of ice in the deep freeze in advance and make sure that several corkscrews and bottle openers are handy on the drinks table.

One bottle opener is no use; it will never be there when it is wanted.

The last drink you must remember is coffee — lots of it, good and strong. After midnight keep a pot steaming on the stove: your guests will appreciate it whether they have been drinking earlier or not. It is good to set out for home with a warm glow on a chilly New Year's morning, and coffee is the perfect drink for that.

Toasts

Mine, and most of our fortunes, tonight,
shall be, — drunk to bed.

Antony and Cleopatra, William Shakespeare

The simplest, most common and most appropriate New Year toast of all is:

A guid New Year to ane an' a',
And mony may ye see.

or in standard English:

A good New Year to one and all,
And many may you see.

If you feel a bit more jingoistic try:

Here's tae us. Wha's like us.

adding this line if you like:

Damn few, and they're a' deid (1)

(1) Dead

Or you can use this simple well-tried Scottish toast:

Lang may yer lum reek!

It means simply, 'Long may your chimney smoke' and it remains ever popular even in these days of fewer coal fires and central heating!

My father loved to puzzle strangers with this toast, which took a couple of drinks to work out:

> *Here's to all those that I love.*
> *Here's to all those that love me.*
> *And here's to all those that love those that I love,*
> *And all those that love those that love me.*

A toast worth memorising is this neat little one:

> *It's guid to be merry an' wise,*
> *It's guid to be honest and true,*
> *It's guid to be aff wi' the auld love,*
> *Afore ye be on wi' the new!*

This one came from my cousin Allan Ramsay from Ayr.

> *May the best you've ever seen*
> *Be the worst you'll ever see.*
> *May the moose ne'er lea'e your mealpoke (mealbag)*
> *Wi' a teardrop in its e'e.*
> *May ye aye be hale and hearty*
> *Till ye're aul' enough tae dee.*
> *May ye aye be just as happy*
> *As I wish ye aye tae be.*

The Jacobites knew about loyalty to the end, even after the Cause was lost. They provide us with a couple of toasts which are gems:

> *Weel may we a' be,*
> *Ill may we never see;*
> *Here's to the King*
> *And the gude companie.*
> *Here's a health to them that's away,*
> *Here's a health to them that's away,*
> *Here's a health to them that were here shortsyne,*
> *An' canna be here today.*

This Hogmanay toast comes from the Shetland Islands:

> *Yule gude an' Yule gear*
> *Follow da troo da year.*

In Gaelic the usual toast is:

> *Slainte mhor* (pronounced, Slanje vahr) — *Good health.*

or

> *Bliadha Sona* (pronounced, Bleeatha sona) — *A Happy New Year.*

A Gaelic blessing for the New Year, taken from *Carmina Gadelica* is:

> *Gu'm beannaicheadh Dia an t-fhardach,*
> *Eadar Chlach, us chuaille, us chrann,*
> *Eadar bhithe, bhliochd, us aodach,*
> *Slainte dhaoin bhi daonnan ann.*

In English this means:

> *May God bless the home,*
> *Stone, implements and beam,*
> *Food, drink and clothing.*
> *May the people in it always be healthy.*

Across the Border in the northern counties of England there are charming New Year toasts. Perhaps some of these might be imported into Scotland to add to our Hogmanay lore. From just across the River Tweed comes a wassailers' toast:

> *Wassail, wassail, all over the town,*
> *Our toast it is white, our ale it is brown.*
> *Our bowl it is made of a maplin tree,*
> *We be good fellas all.*
> *I drink to thee.*

Moving southwards into County Durham one finds an old toast which deserves to be remembered:

> *Happy New Year t' ye!*
> *God send ye plenty!*
> *Where ye have one pound note,*
> *I wish ye may have twenty!*

In Yorkshire, where first-footers are Lucky Birds, the greeting by new arrivals was:

*I wish you health and strength
and a Happy New Year.
Please may I be the Lucky Bird here?*

The Songs

Music, when soft voices die,
Vibrates in the memory —

Song, Percy Bysshe Shelley

A Guid New Year...that's the wish on everybody's lips as the old year fades into the new. Nearly every Scot knows that the greeting can be sung, but few know more than the first couple of lines. It is worth memorising at least the first and last verses to sing at midnight on Hogmanay, or if you are hosting a party you could copy the words out for your guests. That way they will not dry up in mid-chorus.

'Auld Lang Syne' is sung as an ending to every Scottish event from a Burns Supper to a St Andrews Night ceilidh, with the whole company linking hands in a circle at the appropriate moment. Auld lang syne simply means 'A Long Time Ago', but Scots find it a very special reminder of their roots, their homeland and their traditions. Above all, *Auld Lang Syne* is a song of long remembered friendship and kinship.

We sing Robert Burns's version of *Auld Lang Syne*, but the song goes back beyond his time. Burns took an old song and infused it with his own genius, linking remembrance of times past with hope for the future. The whole world recognises this, and has adopted it as a universal song of parting.

When the time comes for *Auld Lang Syne* everyone should gather in a circle, but don't link hands until the last verse. At the words, *'And there's a hand my trust fiere. And gie's a hand o' thine'* all should cross arms and link hands with their neighbours. For the final chorus the tempo is speeded up and the singers move towards the centre of the room and out again, still holding hands, but keeping time to the quickening pace of the song. The song and the party finish with a glorious flourish, in which the words sung are often changed to *'We'll meet again some ither night for auld lang syne.'* That's not what Robert Burns wrote, but it is permissible.

Please, English revellers, try hard to sing *'auld lang syne'* with an 's' sound as in 'signpost' and not *'auld lang zyne'* with a 'z' as in 'resign'. And Scots, don't sing *'for the sake of auld lang syne'*, Burns's words are *'for auld lang syne'*.

A GUID NEW YEAR

Words: Peter Livingstone
Music: Alex Hume

A guid new year to ane an' a'
An' mony may ye see,
An' during a' the years to come
O happy may ye be.
An' may ye ne'er hae cause to mourn,
To sigh or shed a tear.
To ane an' a baith great an' sma'
A hearty guid New year.

CHORUS
A guid New Year to ane an' a'
An' mony may ye see,
An' during a' the years to come
O happy may ye be.

O time flies past, he winna wait,
My friend for you or me,
He works his wonders day by day
And onward still doth flee.
O wha can tell when ilka ane
I see sae happy here
Will meet again and merry be
Anither guid New year.

CHORUS
A guid New Year...

We twa ha'e baith been happy lang.
We ran about the braes.
In yon wee cot beneath the tree
We spent our early days.
We ran about the burnie's side
The spot will aye be dear,
An' those that used to meet us there
We'll think on mony a year.

CHORUS
A guid New Year...

Noo let us hope our years may be
As guid as they ha'e been,
And trust we ne'er again may see
The sorrows we ha'e seen.
And let us wish that ane an' a'
Our friends baith far an' near
May aye enjoy in times to come
A hearty guid New year.

CHORUS
A guid New Year..

AULD LANG SYNE

Words: Robert Burns
Music: Traditional

Should auld acquaintance be forgot,
And never brought to mind?
Should auld acquaintance be forgot,
And auld lang syne?

CHORUS
For auld lang syne, my dear,
For auld lang syne,
We'll tak a cup o' kindness yet
For auld lang syne!

And surely ye'll be your pint stowp, (1)
And surely I'll be mine'
And we'll tak a cup o kindness yet,
For auld lang syne!

CHORUS
For auld lang syne...

We twa hae run about the braes,
And pou'd(2) the gowans(3) fine,
But we've wander'd mony a weary fit,
Sin auld lang syne.

CHORUS
For auld lang syne...

We twa hae paidl'd(4) in the burn,
Frae morning sun till dine,(5)
But seas between us braid(6) hae roar'd
Sin auld lang syne.

1) tankard; (2) pulled; (3) large daisies; (4) paddled; (5) dinnertime; (6) broad

Auld Lang Syne

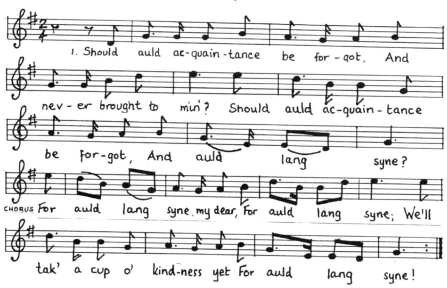

1. Should auld ac-quain-tance be for-got, And
nev-er brought to min'? Should auld ac-quain-tance
be for-got, And auld lang syne?

CHORUS For auld lang syne, my dear, For auld lang syne; We'll
tak' a cup o' kind-ness yet For auld lang syne!

CHORUS
For auld lang syne...

And there's a hand, my trusty fiere,
And gie's a hand o' thine.
And we'll tak a right guid-willie waught, (7),
For auld lang syne.

CHORUS
For auld lang syne, my dear,
For auld lang syne,
We'll tak a cup o' kindness yet,
For auld lang syne.

(7) good swig of drink

The Morning After

But he who drinks just what he likes,
And getteth half-seas over,
Will live until he die perhaps,
And then lie down in clover.

Traditional song: Come, Landlord,
Fill The Flowing Bowl

There are few places in the world as empty at a Scottish town centre on the morning of 1 January. It gives the impression that the whole country is suffering from a great national hangover — and for quite a sizeable section of the population that may well be true.

How to cope with it then? Avoidance is best, but not always possible. After all, few people set out to overindulge; intoxication just creeps over them and by the time they are in line for a hungover morning after, they are probably not in a state to realise it! It seems very unfair, but that's a fact of life at Hogmanay!

BEFORE AND DURING THE PARTY

Hangover cures start the night before by drinking with care, in moderation, always with food, and paving the stomach in advance for what's coming to it. Lining the stomach before the party starts with a pint of milk: the fat will slow the absorption of the alcohol. Don't drink on an empty stomach and eat while you drink; nibble canapes, nuts, crisps, crackers, cheese, anything. Don't mix your drinks too much: everybody knows grape and grain should not be mixed, but be especially careful about spirits and sparkling wine.

Darker, heavier drinks, by and large, induce mightier hangovers than those which contain fewer colouring and flavouring elements. The reason is that they contain fewer cogeners, which is the name given to these secondary products which help to determine colour, flavour and power to intoxicate. As a guide, lighter coloured drinks leave less of a hangover than darker ones. Here is a very rough 'league table':

    Gin
    Vodka
    White wines
    Lager
    Red wines
    Oak-aged wines
    Dark beers
    Whisky
    Dark spirits
    Port

During the party drink water as well as alcohol — hosts should provide spring or mineral water on the dinner table or discreetly alongside the alcoholic drinks at the bar. Take a glass of alcoholic drink, turn about with one of water and you shouldn't suffer too badly next day.

AFTER THE PARTY

Don't despair if you have not observed the above rules. Before going to bed, drink a pint or preferably two pints of cold water. That will reduce dehydration and flush out hangover-inducing agents that may linger in the body. You may have to get up several times during the night, but console yourself with the thought that the alcohol would have had you up anyway.

THE MORNING AFTER

If you still feel rough in the morning, continue the water cure, or drink fruit juice to which you can add vitamin B, aspirin, or honey. Strong black coffee and a walk in the fresh air will also help.

Of course there are proprietary products on the market designed to make you feel better, ranging from Alka Seltzer, which I find particularly good, and Beecham's Resolve to such restoratives as a glass of Fernet Branca or Underberg.

THE HAIR OF THE DOG

The hair of the dog may not be recommended by your doctor, but at least it will ease 're-entry' into the world. However, don't become so carried away that you find yourself back to the state in which you left the party. If you must have the hair of the dog, make it just one wee hair!

Brandy is good for the morning after. Mix it with orange juice, or with a liqueur and Fernet Branca in equal proportions.

If you are still not on your feet, the only remedy is traditional Scottish morning after reviver, the Hogmanannie. Here is how to make it:

Separate the yolks and whites of two eggs. Beat the yolks with two tablespoons of caster sugar and two tablespoons of cream. Beat the egg whites separately until fairly stiff. Add four double measures of whisky to the yolk mixture, beat in the whites and serve.

That should be sufficient to set the whole family up for the day!

And now it's back to work!

Yule's come and Yule's gone,
Ane we hae feasted weel;
Sae Jock maun to his flail again,
And Jenny to her wheel.

The Book of Days
Robert Chambers

Appendix I
Recipes

FOOD FOR THE HOGMANAY CAKE TRAY

BLACK BUN (SCOTCH CURRANT BUN)

Black Bun was a traditional cake baked specially for Twelfth Night. It became a New Year delicacy and Hogmanay would not be Hogmanay without it.

This was my mother's recipe which she made right up to the eighty-

eighth and last, year of her life. She made it gloriously rich and moist as a pudding, but occasionally she became so carried away that by the time she came to add the cayenne pepper she overdid it. Go lightly on the cayenne.

For the Pastry Case
8 oz (225g) plain flour
¼ tsp salt
4 oz (125g) margarine
cold water to mix

Sieve flour and salt. Rub in butter and mix in water to make a stiff dough. Roll out very thin. Put to one side while you make up the filling.

For the Filling
8 oz (225g) plain flour
2 oz (50g) soft brown sugar
2 oz (50g) ground almonds
1 tsp mixed spice
1 tsp cinnamon
1 tsp ground ginger
pinch cayenne pepper
½ tsp baking soda
½ tsp cream of tartar
1 lb (450g) currants
1 lb (450g) raisins
1 lb (450g) sultanas
6 oz (175g) mixed peel
2 oz (50g) chopped almonds
4 eggs (separate yolk and white of one)
buttermilk to mix
brandy

Grease two 2 lb loaf tins or one large tin. Sieve flour and mix in the sugar, ground almonds, mixed spice, cinnamon, ground ginger, cayenne pepper, baking soda and cream of tartar. Stir in the currants, raisins, sultanas, candied peel and chopped almonds. Fold in beaten eggs and buttermilk until mixture is soft and moist. Lastly add brandy.

Use two-thirds of the pastry to line the prepared tin(s), wetting the edges where pastry joins. Pack fruit mixture into the lined tin, filling in corners and smoothing top until it is level. Brush over top of fruit mixture with white of egg. Place remainder of pastry on top of fruit, being careful to seal edges. Brush with beaten egg or milk. Prick with knitting needle right to bottom of tin. Pinch round edges to decorate.

Bake in slow oven at 150 deg C (300 deg F) Gas Mark 2 for 2½ to 3 hours. If the bun browns too quickly, cover with foil until ready.

SHORTBREAD

Shortbread is synonymous with Scotland, not only at Hogmanay when it is a favourite first-footing present as well as the most likely cake which you will be offered when first-footing. It comes as fingers or in rounds divided into triangular slices known as Petticoat Tails — a corruption of the French petites gatelles or 'little cakes'. It keeps well in an airtight tin.

My sister, Margaret, says there are two secrets to making good shortbread: the best of ingredients and cold hands, and her shortbread always wins high praise at New Year parties and prizes at shows. She says it's simple to make: others believe it's an art!

8 oz (225g) butter
4 oz (125g) caster sugar
12 oz (350g) plain flour

Cream butter and sugar. Add flour and mix well, but don't allow it to become oily. Divide mixture into four pieces. Knead into a round or shape in a shortbread mould. Place on baking paper or on a flat baking tray. Prick all over with a fork and pinch the edges with the thumb and first finger. Cook for at least 1 hour in a slow oven at 140 deg C (275

deg F) Gas Mark 1. When cooked, dust with caster sugar and cut immediately. Allow to cool thoroughly.

CHRISTMAS CAKE (PLUM CAKE)

We always called this Christmas cake: my wife's family, who hail
from Northern Ireland, call it plum cake. The recipe on both sides of the
water is much the same. This is my mother's:

11 oz (300g) plain flour
8 oz (225g) sultanas
12 oz (350g) raisins
8 oz (225g) currants
2 oz (50g) cherries
1 oz (25g) mixed peel
3 oz (75g) ground or chopped almonds
½ tsp baking powder
8 oz (225g) butter
8 oz (225g) caster sugar
1 tbs black treacle
6 eggs
1 tbs sherry or brandy if liked
Grease and line a 7 inch tin.

Mix all dry ingredients in a large bowl. Beat butter and sugar to a
cream in another bowl and add eggs, treacle, milk and brandy to it gradually. Add dry ingredients and mix thoroughly. Place mixture in tin,
hollowing out the centre a little. Tie a strip of foil round the tin and bake
in oven at 150 deg C (300 deg F) Gas Mark 2 for 2 hours or until cooked.
If surface browns too quickly, cover with foil.

CHERRY CAKE

This was a great favourite at New Year because it was less rich than
most of the other cakes in the Ne'erday cake basket. Mother often cut
her cherry cake in half as soon as it cooled in order to make sure that it
was a success. If it had gone wrong and the cherries had sunk to the

bottom we rejoiced because she baked another one and we were allowed to eat the rejected one for tea that night!

6 oz (175g) margarine
6 oz (175g) caster sugar
3 eggs (size 3)
3 oz (75g) plain flour
3 oz (75g) self raising flour
2 oz (50g) ground almonds
6 oz (175g) glacé cherries
1 tbs hot water
Grease and line a 7 inch tin.

Cream butter and sugar. Add beaten eggs. Fold in flour and ground almonds. Halve cherries, dust with flour and add to mixture. Stir in hot water. Pour mixture into tin, spreading it well. Bake in oven at 170 deg C (325 deg F) Gas Mark 3 for 1½ hours or until a skewer comes out clean.

SULTANA CAKE

A year-round stand-by cutting cake which also made an appearance at New Year, but this cake is less rich than Christmas Cake.

6 oz (175g) butter or margerine
5 oz (150g) caster sugar
4 eggs
6 oz (175g) plain flour
3 oz (75g) self raising flour
12 oz (350g) sultanas
2 oz (50g) glacé cherries
1 tbs hot water
Grease and line a 7 inch tin.

Cream butter and sugar. Gradually add eggs unbeaten and sieved flour alternately. Stir these in. Add sultanas. Cut cherries into quarters, and dust with flour and add to mixture. If consistency is soft, omit the hot water. Spread mixture evenly in tin, making a slight hollow towards the centre. Bake in moderate oven at 150 deg C (300 deg F) Gas Mark 2 for 2 hours or until ready. Test with a skewer.

SEED CAKE

Old fashioned seed cake was popular throughout the year, but in Edinburgh especially it was frequently included in the cake basket which was handed round to Ne'erday visitors. This tried and tested recipe comes from Jenny Moser.

5 oz (150g) butter or margarine
5 oz (150g) caster sugar
3 eggs
6 oz (175g) self raising flour
2 oz (50g) ground almonds
2 tsp caraway seeds

Cream margarine and sugar until light and fluffy. Add beaten eggs a little at a time. (If necessary, add a little flour to prevent curdling.) Mix carraway seeds with flour and fold into creamed mixture. Place mixture into greased 7 inch or 2 lb loaf tin. Bake 1 1/2 hours at 180 deg C (350 deg F) Gas Mark 4 until golden brown and firm to touch.

OATCAKES

At New Year oatcakes were spiked up with caraway, sowans or even cinnamon, and were eaten with a special Yule kebbuck of cheese.

The best oatcake baker in our family (and probably in Ayrshire) was cousin Marian. Her oatcakes were thin as paper, crisp and delicate — and their flavour was out of this world. Rolling out and baking oatcakes is an art which takes time to master, but it is well worth persevering. Marian's recipe came from an old Galloway shepherd's wife half a century ago.

1 teacup oatmeal
pinch of salt
¼ tsp baking soda
1 tsp melted bacon fat
¼ teacup hot water

Mix the meal, salt and baking soda. Add bacon fat and water carefully to make a soft dough. Turn on to a baking board and sprinkle with oatmeal. Knead well and roll out very thinly into a large circle. Keep sprinkling with dry oatmeal to prevent sticking. Cut into quarters or traditional three farls and place carefully on a hot girdle. When the edges begin to curl up, turn and cook other side, or (better still) remove from the girdle, rub in more oatmeal and bake second side in front of an open fire or in the oven.

SOUP

SCOTCH BROTH

If you really want to turn the clock back serve Sheep's Head Broth, but good, plain Scotch Broth is a lot less bother and it fills a gap at Ne'erday just as well. Mother made it so thick you could have plastered a wall with it and as children we carefully removed the beans and peas to eat with our potatoes. Delicious!

4 pints (2 litres) water
1 lb (450g) neck of mutton or a bone
2 oz (50g) barley soaked overnight
2 oz (50g) dried beans soaked overnight
2 oz (50g) dried peas soaked overnight
1 onion
1 carrot
1 leek
1 small turnip (swede)

1 cabbage heart
salt
pepper

Place mutton, barley, beans and peas in pot with water. Bring to boil and add onion, leek, carrot and turnip cut in small pieces. Simmer gently until vegetables are soft — at least 2 hours. When almost ready add shredded cabbage heart. Skim off fat, adjust seasoning to taste, remove meat and serve.

I often make broth with Knorr chicken stock cubes instead of mutton and it tastes delicious.

MAIN COURSES

STEAK PIE

Nobody makes a better Steak Pie (or rather Steak and Kidney Pie) than my wife. The Scots tended to make their New Year pie only with beefsteak, eked out in poorer homes with lumps of sausage meat. I like the New Year pie with lots of kidney and here's how my wife makes it.

Flaky Pastry
8 oz (225g) plain flour
½ tsp salt
6 oz (175g) butter (or equal amounts margarine and lard)
½ pint (275 ml) water
1 tsp lemon juice

Sieve flour and salt into mixing bowl. Beat fat on a plate (if using margarine and lard make sure they are mixed well) and rub a quarter of it into the flour. Add water and lemon juice and mix to an elastic dough. Roll out to rectangular shape and place another quarter of the fat in small pieces over two thirds of the rolled pastry. Fold ends of pastry in, turn through 90 degrees and seal ends. Re-roll and repeat process twice until all fat is used up. Let pastry rest in refrigerator until required. Roll out and fold twice, then use.

Filling
1½lbs (600g) stewing steak, or steak and
kidney in the proportion you prefer
2 oz (50g) seasoned flour
2 tbsp oil
1 onion
½ pint (275 ml) beef stock
mixed herbs
salt
pepper

Cut steak and kidney into cubes and roll in seasoned flour. Chop onion and fry in oil. Remove onion from pan and fry meat until browned all over. This is best done carefully, a few pieces at a time. Add stock, mixed herbs and seasoning. Simmer until meat is tender. Place meat in pie dish with pie funnel in centre. Roll out pastry and cut a half inch strip to place round the lip of the pie dish. Wet this strip and place pastry lid on top. Press edges down gently. Trim edge. Decorate with pastry leaves and make small hole in centre. Brush with beaten egg or milk.

Cook in hot oven at 220 deg C (425 deg F) Gas Mark 7 for 20 minutes, then reduce heat 180 deg C (350 deg F) Gas Mark 4 for about 20 minutes. Be careful not to let pastry overcook.

TIBBIES'S IRISH STEW

Irish Stew is a perfect dish for supper after a winter's day spent outdoors, walking on the hills, shooting, playing sport or just spectating. It is even tastier eaten in the open air at a picnic. Just make sure it keeps piping hot!

My friend Isabelle (Tibbie) Shaw, who grew up in the Tibbie Shiels Inn in the Yarrow Valley, gave me this recipe which her mother used for

New Year shooting parties at the inn. Here it is in her own words. You will need:

tatties
neck or breast of mutton
onions
carrots
water or stock (chicken)
salt and pepper
large knob of butter
chopped chives for decoration
celery or celery salt (optional)

Quantities can vary according to what is available and the size of the party. Just include amount of each that you would use if serving as a meal of meat and accompanying vegetables, but allowing some extra potato. Put into a lidded earthenware dish the cut-up mutton coated with seasoned flour. Cut potatoes, carrots and onions small and place in dish with knob of butter. Pour in stock or water, not quite covering ingredients. Celery salt may be added if liked, or a small stick of celery cut up. Place in a medium oven at 180 deg C (350 F) Gas Mark 4 to start with and then reduce to a low oven at 150 deg C (300 deg F) Gas Mark 2. Cook for 2 hours. The liquid should all be taken up by the end of cooking. Before serving, add chopped chives sprinkled on top.

CHUMP CHOPS WITH PORTER

This was James Hogg's favourite dish and consequently was served at the Tibbie Shiels Inn at Ne'erday. The recipe comes from Isabelle Shaw.

1-2 lamb chops per person
onions
Guinness

Marinade chops overnight in porter (Guinness or other stout) to which chopped onions have been added.

In the old days this dish was marinaded and cooked in a large, flat, iron hanging pan with a lid, which hung over a slow peat fire on the 'swee' at the Tibbie Shiels Inn. The mixture was allowed to cook until tender. The liquid should all be taken up by the end of the cooking. It was served with rowan jelly, curly kale and baked potatoes.

ROASTED GOOSE

Forget turkey or chicken — give the family a fine roasted goose as traditionally Scottish as New Year itself. Mary Campbell, who has spent most of her life in the Highlands and now lives at Evanton in Ross-shire, gave me this recipe.

Choose a young bird, about 10 to 15lbs (4½-7kg) and prepare it as you would any large fowl. Stuff it with a dried fruit stuffing instead of the more usual sage and onion stuffing because herbs spoil the goose's own delicious flavour.

For the stuffing you will need:
6oz (175g) white breadcrumbs
4oz (125g) dried apricots*
1 apple (chopped)
1tbs chopped parsley
2oz (50g) butter
6oz (175g) onions
juice and grated rind of a small orange
salt
pepper
1 small egg
*Fruit mixture can be varied — try sultanas or stoned prunes.

To make the stuffing, melt the butter and mix well with all the ingredients.

Set the stuffed goose on a rack in a roasting tin to collect the juices during cooking. Goose does not require basting. Roast at 200 deg C (400 deg F) Gas Mark 6 for the first 20 minutes and reduce to 180 deg C (350 deg F) Gas Mark 4 for the remainder of the time. Allow 25 minutes per pound cooking time.

Goose fat is simply the best and there will be plenty of it. Once cooked, pour it off and freeze it in handy containers. A spoonful will enrich stir fries and in the old days, goose grease was rubbed on the chest to prevent winter ailments.

Serve with rowan or aloe and apple jelly.

DESSERTS

CLOOTIE DUMPLING

Clootie Dumpling was for birthdays as well as Ne'erday and we ate it with a knife and fork, but never with cream as a pudding. It was delicious fried for breakfast the following morning and we took a slice to school for our midday 'piece'. Anybody with a piece of dumpling was the envy of the whole playground. This was mother's recipe.

1 lb (450g) self raising flour
6 oz (175g) sugar
1 level tsp baking soda
1 level tsp cream of tartar
2 tsp cinnamon
2 tsp mixed spice
8 oz (225g) seedless raisins
8 oz (225g) sultanas
6 oz (175g) shredded suet or margarine
4 eggs
1 tbs syrup

Mix all the dry ingredients in a bowl. Rub in margarine or suet, then add eggs and syrup. Mix with milk or water to make a soft dough. Dampen a square of cotton well in hot water, and lay it flat on a table. Sprinkle generously with flour and put mixture on to it. Gather the corners of the cloth together and tie with string. Be careful to leave room for the dumpling to swell, but not too much room. Have a pot ready with as much boiling water as will cover the dumpling. Place an old plate in the bottom of the pot to keep the dumpling from sticking. Lower dumpling into the water and boil steadily for about 4 hours. Turn onto a plate, removing the cloth gently. Put the dumpling in a cool oven for a short time to dry off.

SCOTCH TRIFLE

Why it should be called Scotch trifle I cannot imagine, unless it is simply because it's gorgeously sweet and the Scots must have the sweetest tooth in Europe! This version certainly was such a favourite with visitors at home that it was always served at parties and at Hogmanay. It should be made in a deep, cut-glass bowl to show the trifle in its splendid colours: that way it is a feast for the eye as well as for the palate.

½ pint (275 mls) of made up strawberry or raspberry jelly
sponge fingers
strawberry/raspberry jam
1 glass sherry
juice from fruit
1 large tin pears (drained)
½ pint custard (275 ml) (not very thick)
1 large tin peaches (drained)
½ pint (275 ml) orange jelly
whipped cream
angelica, hundreds and thousands, nuts or glacé cherries to deco-
    rate

Let the strawberry or raspberry jelly set in a deep, cut-glass bowl. Spread the sponge fingers with jam and lay them on top of the set jelly. Pour the sherry and a little of the juice from the tinned fruit over to moisten them. Set a layer of pear slices over the sponge, then a thin layer of custard, followed with a layer of peach slices. Pour orange jelly over that. Leave in fridge to set. Just before serving, spread whipped cream on top and decorate with angelica, hundreds and thousands, nuts or glacé cherries.

CREAM OF ATHOLL BROSE

Atholl Brose (recipe: page 147) is a splendid drink for a festive occasion, but it can form the basis of a delicious, wickedly rich dessert.

Atholl Brose
whipped cream
fine oatmeal
nutmeg

Make Atholl Brose in usual way. Place three tablespoons of it in a stemmed glass for each person. Lightly mix in whipped cream. sprinkle lightly with fine oatmeal and nutmeg. A little very finely grated lemon peel makes a delicious variation.

DRINKS

HET PINT

The Het Pint was a real warmer for first-footers a century and more ago. It was really a kind of mulled ale which people carried in a copper kettle and offered to friends (and strangers) they met on their first-footing rounds. This Victorian recipe comes from Robert Chambers's Book of Days and belongs to an age when people had more time and a totally different choice of ingredients available. I include it for interest only, but you could try Meg Dods' recipe which follows this as a welcoming punch for your party. Just adapt it to suit your budget.

'Simmer a small quantity of the following spices in a tea-cupful of water, viz:- Cardamums, cloves, nutmeg, mace, ginger, cinnamom, and coriander. When done, put the spice to two, four, or six bottles of port, sherry, or madeira, with one pound and a half of fine loaf sugar (pounded) to four bottles, and set all on the fire in a clean bright saucepan; meanwhile, have yolks of 12 and the whites of 6 eggs well whisked up in it. Then, when the spiced and sugared wine is a little warm, take out one teacupful; and so on for three or four cups; after which,

when it boils, add the whole of the remainder, pouring it in gradually, and stirring it briskly all the time, so as to froth it. The moment a fine froth is obtained, toss in 12 fine soft roasted apples, and send it up hot. Spices for each bott of wine:- 10 grains of mace, 46 grains of cloves, 37 grains of cardamums, 28 grains of cinnamon, 12 grains of nutmeg, 48 grains of ginger, 49 grains of coriander seeds.'

Het Pint from the cookery book published in 1826 *The Cook and Housewife's Manual* by Mistress Margaret Dods is rather easier. You will require:

4 pints mild ale
3 eggs
½ pint Scotch whisky
nutmeg
sugar to taste

Mistress Dods's method was: grate a nutmeg into two quarts of mild ale, and bring it to the point of boiling. Mix a little cold ale with sugar necessary to sweeten this, and three eggs, taking care that they do not curdle. Put in a half pint of Scotch whisky, and bring it once more nearly to the boil and then briskly pour it from one vessel into another till it becomes smooth and bright.

MULLED ALE

Heat the ale with the rind and juice of one lemon in a pan, adding a sprinkling of nutmeg and a little sugar to take away to tartness of the ale. Serve hot from a large bowl.

ATHOLL BROSE

Atholl Brose nowadays is offered on special occasions all year round. It cannot fail to be delicious since it blends the best Scottish ingredients — oatmeal, whisky, cream, honey and eggs. Be warned, it's rich and very sweet!

This is my late brother-in-law, Alec Gregor's, recipe, used by him in Africa for years. He could never tell how much it made since he and the family tested and tasted it so often and so thoroughly while it matured that there usually was only one bottle left by Hogmanay. All the 'shrinkage' is not due to illicit tasting, however; I find it settles to about half the quantity as it matures.

1 bottle Scotch whisky
½ pint (10 fl oz) double cream
1 lb (450g) clear honey
whites of 6 eggs
1 handful of oatmeal (fine ground)

Soak oatmeal in Scotch whisky. Beat egg whites until stiff, then fold cream into them. Add the honey. Very slowly blend in the whisky and oatmeal. Pour into bottles and store for 1 week, shaking — and no doubt tasting! — occasionally.

GINGER WINE

Ginger Wine or Cordial is an essential part of every child's and every teetotaller's Hogmanay. It may not be alcoholic, but it can carry a kick. However, if you make your own you can reduce or increase the quantity of ginger to taste. This is a recipe from my sister, Amelia.

To make 1 gallon approximately you will need:

2 oz (50g) root ginger
2 lemons
2 oranges
1 gallon (3.8 litres) water
3½ lbs (1.5 kg) sugar
small pinch of cayenne pepper (optional)

Break the ginger up, using rather less if a milder brew is wanted, and boil it with 1 gallon of water and the rind of the oranges and lemons. If you want a ginger wine that will really toast the tonsils add a small pinch of cayenne pepper during boiling. Strain the liquid into a container holding the sugar. Add the juice of the lemons and oranges. Strain and bottle.

Appendix II
Coping With Spills

Disasters happen before, during and after the best run parties, and the secret is to be prepared. Don't wait for the wine to be spilt on the carpet — have the remedy ready. We keep a 'help-line' shelf beside the washing machine to cope with daily disasters, and it is also our party help-line. This includes proprietary dry cleaning solvent containing the stain removal standby, carbon tetrachloride. Also useful would be some methylated spirit, borax, glycerine, hydrogen peroxide, household ammonia, salt, biological detergent and carpet shampoo. Stain removers called Stain Devils are available for many specific stains such as ink or blood, but favourite all-round stand by is Vanish, a multi-purpose stain stick which works wonders with all kinds of disasters to fabrics.

Read the washing instructions on the garment before tackling a stain and if uncertain how the remedy will affect a fabric try it on a small area which is not seen (a hem, for example). If still unsure, seek professional help.

The following are remedies for the main disasters you are likely to encounter on Hogmanay.

BURNS

Better avoided than remedied: have plenty of ashtrays around the house, or better still, dishes containing sand to hold cigarette ends.

FURNITURE: rub light burns well with good furniture polish. Serious burns, seek professional help.

CARPETS or UPHOLSTERY: rub with glycerine or hydrogen

peroxide, then sponge gently with diluted carpet shampoo. Blot well and allow to dry.

FABRICS: if lightly scorched, run cold water on the mark; otherwise, rub with glycerine and wash as usual, or soak in diluted hydrogen peroxide. Non-washables or more serious marks should be left to a professional dry cleaner.

CANDLE WAX

CARPETS and UPHOLSTERY: pick off as much as you can, then iron gently with blotting paper over the stain.

FABRICS: pick off, then place stained material face down between sheets of blotting paper iron with a warm iron. Methylated spirit will help to take away a stain left by coloured wax. Non-washables: take to dry cleaner.

COFFEE

CARPETS and UPHOLSTERY: the soda siphon used to be the thing, but there are few of these around these days, so sponge with diluted carpet shampoo. Repeat if necessary, finally rinsing with cold water.

FABRICS: wash with plenty of cold water immediately, then wash in detergent. If stain dries, soak in detergent and wash. Non-washables: try the dry cleaner.

CREAM/MILK

CARPETS and UPHOLSTERY: wipe off excess, dab with a grease solvent or sponge with diluted carpet shampoo. Rinse well.

FABRICS: wipe off, rinse in cold water, the wash with soapy water. Non-washables: use proprietary stain remover or take to dry cleaner.

FOOD/GRAVY

CARPETS and UPHOLSTERY: dab over with cold water and then detergent, sponge with diluted carpet shampoo, then rinse.

FABRICS: soak in cold water, then in detergent. Heavy stains may need a second treatment.

LIPSTICK

CARPETS and UPHOLSTERY: scrape off as much as possible, rub glycerine in and wash with diluted carpet shampoo. Rinse, blot dry.

FABRICS: rub in dry-cleaning solvent, methylated spirit, or glycerine (whichever is available) and wash in usual way.

TEA

CARPETS and UPHOLSTERY: sponge with lots of warm water, blot and repeat with diluted carpet shampoo.

FABRICS: soak in detergent solution and wash as usual. Non-washables: ask a dry cleaner.

VOMIT

CARPETS and UPHOLSTERY: wipe off quickly with a cloth or tissues and sponge with lots of warm water. Sponge with diluted carpet shampoo containing a few drops of household ammonia. Rinse well and blot dry.

FABRICS: Wipe off as much as possible then wash in warm biological detergent with a few drops of disinfectant or white vinegar in it. Non-washables: wipe off garment and leave to a professional dry cleaner.

WINE (RED)

Some people swear by lots of white wine poured on the stain immediately. Alternatively you can try:

CARPETS and UPHOLSTERY: blot up as much as possible or pour lots of salt on stain. Sponge with plenty of warm water.

FABRICS: blot or (if on a tablecloth) cover stain with plenty of salt. Sponge with tepid water. Borax is good for stubborn stains. Non-washables: take to a dry cleaner as quickly as possible.

WINE (WHITE)

CARPETS and UPHOLSTERY: blot well and sponge with cool water. Dry off and wash with diluted carpet shampoo.

FABRICS: blot and soak in cold water, wash. Non-washables: blot dry and take to a dry cleaner.